W9-AEA-205

Gramley Library
Salem College
Winston-Salem, NC 27108

The Garland Library of Medieval Literature

General Editors
James J. Wilhelm, Rutgers University
Lowry Nelson, Jr., Yale University

Literary Advisors
Ingeborg Glier, Yale University
Frede Jensen, University of Colorado
Sidney M. Johnson, Indiana University
William W. Kibler, University of Texas
Norris J. Lacy, Washington University
Fred C. Robinson, Yale University
Aldo Scaglione, New York University

Art Advisor
Elizabeth Parker McLachlan, Rutgers University

Music Advisor
Hendrik van der Werf, Eastman School of Music

Kassia
The Legend, the Woman and Her Work

edited and translated by
ANTONÍA TRIPOLITIS

Volume 84
Series A
GARLAND LIBRARY OF MEDIEVAL LITERATURE

Garland Publishing, Inc.

New York & London

1992

Gramley Library
Salem College
Winston-Salem, NC 27108

Copyright © 1992 by Antonía Tripolitis
All rights reserved

Library of Congress Cataloging-in-Publication Data

Tripolitis, Antonía, 1934-
    Kassia : the legend, the woman, and her work / edited and translated by
Antonía Tripolitis.
        p.   cm. — (Garland library of medieval literature ; v. 84.
Series A)
    Includes bibliographical references.
    ISBN 0-8240-2990-9 (alk. paper)
    1. Kassianē, b. ca. 810—Translations into English.   I. Title.   II. Series:
Garland library of medieval literature ; v. 84.
PA5319.K295A27   1992
881'.02—dc20   92-17422
                                                            CIP

Printed on acid-free, 250-year-life paper
Manufactured in the United States of America

This book is dedicated
to the memory of my mother
at whose knee I first learned
about Kassia

Preface of the General Editors

The Garland Library of Medieval Literature was established to make available to the general reader modern translations of texts in editions that conform to the highest academic standards. All of the translations are originals, and were created especially for this series. The translations usually attempt to render the foreign works in a natural idiom that remains faithful to the originals, although in certain cases we have published more poetic versions.

The Library is divided into two sections: Series A, texts and translations; and Series B, translations alone. Those volumes containing texts have been prepared after consultation of the major previous editions and manuscripts. The aim in the edition has been to offer a reliable text with a minimum of editorial intervention. Significant variants accompany the original, and important problems are discussed in the Textual Notes. Volumes without texts contain translations based on the most scholarly texts available, which have been updated in terms of recent scholarship.

Most volumes contain Introductions with the following features: (1) a biography of the author or a discussion of the problem of authorship, with any pertinent historical or legendary information; (2) an objective discussion of the literary style of the original, emphasizing any individual features; (3) a consideration of sources for the work and its influence; and (4) a statement of the editorial policy for each edition and translation. There is also a Select Bibliography, which emphasizes recent criticism on the works. Critical writings are often accompanied by brief descriptions of their importance. Selective glossaries, indices, and footnotes are included where appropriate.

The Library covers a broad range of linguistic areas, including all of the major European languages. All of the important literary forms and genres are considered, sometimes in anthologies or selections.

The General Editors hope that these volumes will bring the
general reader a closer awareness of a richly diversified area that
has for too long been closed to everyone except those with precise
academic training, an area that is well worth study and reflection.

James J. Wilhelm
Rutgers University

Lowry Nelson, Jr.
Yale University

CONTENTS

INTRODUCTION

Kassia, Kasia, or Kassiane, as she is known liturgically, was a highly gifted ninth-century Byzantine poetess long considered by the Eastern Church as the most distinguished woman hymnographer. One of her hymns on Mary Magdalene, which established her literary fame, is generally considered a masterpiece of Christian Greek poetry. Its performance is the highlight of the Orthos of Holy Wednesday, the daybreak service which corresponds to the Matins in the Western Tradition. It is sung on Holy Tuesday evening, since in the Orthodox tradition, as in Judaism and other ancient religions, the day begins at sunset, and it is found in the Triodion, the Lenten liturgical book. Although the names and works of three other women are known, Kassia's are the only ones included in the ecclesiastical books. She is the only woman mentioned in a fourteenth-century catalog of famous hymnographers compiled by Nicephoros Kallistos Xanthopoulos, a hymnographer and priest in the church of St. Sophia in Constantinople,[1] and the only woman included in the frontpiece of a Triodion, printed in Venice in 1601, which pictures twenty-nine of the Church's great hymnodists.[2] Most of the acknowledged hymnographers whose works are included in the ecclesiastical books were honored by the Church by being elevated to sainthood. Kassia, however, although recognized as a first-rate hymnographer, has been denied canonization.

Tradition and manuscript authority attribute to Kassia forty-nine religious hymns and two hundred sixty-one secular verses in the form of epigrams and gnomic verses or moral sentences. These works are found in numerous manuscripts dating from the eleventh to the sixteenth century and bear the name Kassia, her true name, or Eikasia or Ikasia. Manuscript scholars suggest that Eikasia and Ikasia are copyists' errors that resulted from the annexation of the feminine article "η", a common mistake of scribes. Twenty-three of the forty-nine hymns are considered genuine. Of the other twenty-six, the manuscripts are not always in agreement. In some a hymn may be attributed to Kassia, while in another it might be claimed anonymous or attributed to a male hymnographer.[3] Moreover, Theodoros Prodromos, a twelfth-century literary figure, in his commentaries on the hymns of some of the Church's more famous hymnographers, states that the famous tetraodion, four-ode, canon for Holy Saturday was originally composed by Kassia, but the Church authorities did not think it proper to credit a woman with a hymn that was sung on one of the most important religious festivals. Therefore, it was attributed to the eight-century Bishop of Maiouma in Phoenicia, Cosmas. Later, at the beginning of the tenth century, some phrases in the odes were changed and five additional odes were added to the canon by Bishop Marcus of Hydrous, Italy.[4] The canon exists in the Triodion in its altered form. However, two manuscripts, with dates unknown, found in the library of the Monastery of Mt. Athos and transcribed by Eustratiades, contain the original hymn as it was written by Kassia and they attribute it to her.[5] These two manuscripts are the only extant sources of Kassia's original Easter tetraodion,[6] which is considered one of her best longer works.

Until the manuscript studies of Lambros (1892-94), Krumbacher (1897), Papadapoulos-Kerameus (1901), Tillyard (1911), Mystakides (1926), and Eustratiades (1932), Kassia was not given credit for all her works.[7] To date, except for her famous penitential hymn on Mary Magdalene, very little scholarship has focused on her work.[8] The little that has been done deals with the musical, metric, and melodic composition of her better known religious hymns.[9] In recent years, Kassia has begun to attract the attention of scholars interested in the history and thought of both the Greek and Latin Middle Ages and modern writers and critics interested in the development of Greek literature.[10] Critics of Greek poetry, religious and secular, consider her the most distinguished poetess of the Greek Middle Ages, and claim that throughout the centuries very few women have made as significant a

contribution as did Kassia.[11] Given the acknowledged
importance of her work both for the Greek medieval
period and for later Greek poetry, it is important that
her works be made accessible. The purpose of this
study is to compile, translate and comment on the
extant works of Kassia and provide a biography and
general assessment of this extraordinary woman.

The work is not a study of ninth-century
Byzantium, its history, literature and culture or a
study of the manuscript tradition of Kassia's works.
Both the religious and secular material are from the
manuscript studies mentioned above,[12] and the
ecclesiastical books of the Eastern Church. The
hagiographic material used to explain the hymns,
especially those for little known saints, is based on
those acknowledged works of the Church.

I wish to thank the Rutgers University Research
Council for their generous support in the preparation
of the manuscript. I am also grateful and indebted to
Dr. Joseph P. Consoli of Princeton University Library
and now Humanities Bibliographer at Rutgers University,
without whose resourcefulness and diligence I would not
have been able to obtain much of the needed documents
to make this study possible.

LIFE AND TIMES OF THE AUTHOR

Kassia lived during the last years of the
iconoclastic controversy, a time when the Eastern Roman
Empire was undergoing great agitation in its political
and ecclesiastical matters. The controversy, which
shook the foundation of the Eastern Empire, began in
726 when the emperor Leo III (717-41) issued an edict
abolishing the use of icons and removing them from the
churches, and its repercussions lasted until well into
the tenth century. From the very beginning of the
controversy, it was the women together with the monks
who remained faithful to the Church's tradition, and it
was two imperial women who helped to re-establish the
icons. In 787, after the death of her husband Leo IV
(775-80), Empress Irene first restored the veneration

of icons, although temporarily, and in 843 Empress
Theodora, after the death of her husband Theophilos
(830-42), permanently restored icon worship. The event
was first celebrated on the eleventh of March, 843, the
first Sunday of Lent, and it continues to be celebrated
in the Eastern Greek Church on the first lenten Sunday
as the feast of triumph or orthodoxy.

Women from all classes of Byzantine society,
laywomen and monastics alike, openly defied the
imperial edict. They were persecuted and many suffered
martyrdom. Kassia joined the struggle at a very young
age, while still in her teens. She suffered
persecution and was once beaten with a lash for aiding
imprisoned monks and iconodule exiles.[13]

Little is known about Kassia's life. She was born
of a noble family between 805-810 in Constantinople.
Her father was a Candidatos at the Imperial Court, a
military position of honor conferred upon members of
the aristocratic class. Like many young women of her
social standing, Kassia was privately educated and
received a classical Greek education. In her early
teens, Kassia was influenced by Theodore (759-826), the
abbot of the Studite Monastery in Constantinople and
the indomitable defender of the icons during the
iconoclastic controversy. The correspondence between
Kassia and the abbot reveals that early in life she had
decided to become a nun and asked him for permission to
adopt the monastic life. He would not give her
authorization, but compliments her on her learning and
on the literary skill of the compositions that she had
sent him.[14]

About 830 A.D., Kassia was one of the beautiful
noble women selected to participate in the traditional
bride-show held for the Emperor Theophilus (829-42) to
choose an empress by presenting a golden apple to the
young woman of his choice. Legend claims that
Theophilus, attracted by Kassia's beauty, stopped
before her and, before offering her the golden apple,
said, "Through woman has come all evil." She, without
hesitation, replied, "But also through woman better
things began," implying the regeneration of mankind
through the birth of Christ. Stunned and displeased by
Kassia's bold reply, Theophilus passed her by and
extended the apple to Theodora. According to the

chroniclers of the time, Kassia, rejected by the Emperor, accepted the monastic life and in 843, about the age of thirty-three, founded her own monastery bearing her name on Xerolophos, the seventh hill in Constantinople near the Constantinian Wall. There she lived and spent her remaining days as abbess of the monastery pursuing her literary interests, writing hymns to be sung during the services in her monastery, as well as secular verses. She died sometime during the bitter years of the reign of Michael III (842-67), around 865. It was not unusual in the Byzantine world for individual men and women, lay or ecclesiastical, to establish monasteries. Some, founded by royal or powerful persons, still survive. Often, however, as with Kassia's, the establishment is known only by a chance reference in a monastic's or saint's biography or chronicle.

The account of Kassia's participation in the bride-show of Theophilus is recounted by several chroniclers with slight variations, beginning with Simeon the Logothete in the tenth century. It is one of the most popular legends of the Christian East, and has made Kassia a well known figure of Greek folklore.[15] Some scholars have questioned the historical accuracy of Theophilus' bride-show and the tradition in general. Most scholars, however, and especially the recent studies of W. T. Treadgold,[16] have indicated that both the account of the bride-show and Kassia's attendance at the show are historically true. There is no indisputable proof of the authenticity of the verbal exchange between Kassia and Theophilus that caused her to lose the contest and hence the throne, but the caustic tone and the strong opinions that are revealed in her epigrams and gnomic verses tend to imply that such an exchange might indeed have taken place.

Imperial bride-shows were very popular in Byzantium during the eighth and ninth centuries with the reigning rulers and the general public. Accounts of five such shows that took place between 788 and 882 are recorded in chronicles, hagiography and folklore. The custom was adopted from the oriental monarchies, and introduced to the Byzantine court in 788 by Empress Irene who appears to have been inspired by the account of the bride-show of the Persian King Xerxes (485-65 B.C.), called Ahasuerus, in the Book of Esther (2:2ff.). The shows were discontinued after the reign of Leo VI (886-912). His bride-show of 882 is the last one recorded. Historians believe that the dynastic complications of the tenth and eleventh centuries did not present any opportunities for bride-shows, and after almost two centuries of disuse, the custom was never revived.[17] However, it was adopted by the imperial court of Russia and preserved through the seventeenth century.[18]

Kassia's works show her to be a bright, gifted poet with emotional sensitivity and originality of thought. They also display a deeply religious individual, but one who is very much aware of the secular world and the shortcomings and failures of the individuals in it, about which she has very emphatic views. Her religious poetry reveals her unquestionable faith and belief in God and his ever-present redeeming love and her trust in the intercessions of the saints that she praises. Almost all her hymns end with a prayer for the worshipers and an appeal to Christ, whose redeeming mercy and love she knew was available to all human beings. In general, Kassia's hymns are more original and impressive than those of most of her contemporaries, who adhered to the established hymnographical tradition. Much of their poetry tends to be verbose, lengthy and often unoriginal. It is heavily dependent on Biblical subjects and phraseology. In contrast, her poetry is short and concise; she uses half as many words as her contemporaries to describe the same religious situation. Her vocabulary is usually simple, poignant and dramatic, and she often blends narrative and dramatic elements to produce hymns of vivid imagery and intense religious emotions. A prime example of this is her famous penitential hymn on Mary Magdalene and her celebration hymn on the birth of Christ, When Augustus Reigned. Even the hymns that follow the established hymnographical tradition are shorter and less wordy than those of others.

The secular works of Kassia, consisting mainly of epigrams and gnomic verses, are concerned with a variety of subjects, such as fortune, wealth, luck, woman, stupidity, friendship, social customs and human

habits that she loathed. Her views on these subjects
are expressed in a forceful, frank and often sarcastic
manner. There is no sign of forbearance or of prayer
for the misguided in many of her secular verses, only
disgust and sometimes hate.

SOURCES AND INFLUENCES

Kassia's works can be divided into two main
categories: religious hymns and secular verses. Her
religious works consist of _idiomela troparia_,
independent short laudatory hymns with their own
melodies, many of which Kassia composed herself, and
canons. The _troparion_ is the earliest form of Greek
Christian religious poetry and dates from the fourth
century. _Troparia_ were written for specific feasts of
saints or important religious holidays and are hymns of
praise with a pronounced laudatory and lyrical
character. Many of them have a fixed place in the
liturgy and a particular function.

The canon originated in the last half of the
seventh century and is a hymn-cycle of eight odes,
numbered one and three to nine. There is no second ode
in any canon. The structure of the canon is such
because it was originally designed to accompany the
reading of the nine Scriptural canticles or odes used
in the liturgy of the Matins:

     (1) Song of Moses (Exodus 15:1-19)
     (2) Song of Moses (Deuteronomy 32:1-43)
     (3) Prayer of Hannah (1 Kings [1 Samuel]
          2:1-100)
     (4) Prayer of Habakkuk (Habakkuk 3:1-19)
     (5) Prayer of Isaiah (Isaiah 26:3-10)
     (6) Prayer of Jonah (Jonah 2:3-10)
     (7) Prayer of the Three Holy Children
          (Daniel 3:26-56)
     (8) Song of the Three Holy Children
          (Benedicite: Daniel 3:57-88)
     (9) Song of the Theotokos (Magnificat: Luke
          1:46-55) and the Prayer of Zacharias
          (Benedictus: Luke 1:68-79)

Although the Magnificat and Benedicts are two separate canticles, in the Byzantine liturgy they are treated as a single one. During the eighth century, the second canticle (Deut. 32:1-43) was omitted from the liturgy, except for certain days in Lent, supposedly because of its mournful character. Thus the canons never had an ode numbered two, and although theoretically canons should contain nine odes, in reality they have only eight. The canons of the week days in Lent contain as a rule two, three or four odes. Kassia's canon written for Holy Saturday is, as the name implies, tetraodion--a four-ode canon. Each ode in a canon is made up of a number of metrically identical stanzas or troparia, from three to twenty and sometimes more. The first stanza of each ode is called an heirimos and it sets the musical and metrical pattern for the other stanzas in the ode. In each ode there is generally some reference, direct or indirect, to the Biblical canticle of the same number; e.g., the first ode makes reference to Moses at the Red Sea, the third to that of Hannah, etc. Canons were composed at first for the most solemn religious festivals: Lent, Easter and Pentecost. Later they were written to celebrate the feast or saint of the day or a particular theme, such as repentance, the Savior, the Theotokos or the departed.

Tradition and manuscript authority attribute to Kassia forty-nine religious hymns, forty-seven troparia and two canons--one of 252 verses, On the Departed, her longest work, and the Tetraodion for Holy Saturday. Except for the canon on the departed, they are found in the Menaia and the Triodion, two liturgical books of the Eastern Orthodox Church. The Menaia is a series of twelve volumes, one for each month of the year, from September 1, the beginning of the ecclesiastical year, until August 31. It contains the services for the fixed holidays and saints' days and the special hymns and prayers commemorating them. The Triodion contains the services of the ten weeks preceding Easter, from the Sunday of the Pharisee and the Publican up to and including Holy Saturday. These books received their present form sometime in the ninth century.

The secular works of Kassia consist of epigrams and gnomic verses or moral sentences or maxims. The

Introduction

epigram, a poetic form half-way between epic and lyric
and written in elegiac couplet, iambic trimeter or less
frequently in hexameter, was popular among Greek
writers since the sixth century B.C. Initially it was
used in inscriptions, mostly funerary or dedicatory, on
buildings or other forms of art. In the fourth century
B.C. it developed as independent literature. Although
epigrams continued to be composed for inscriptions,
they were also used as a form of intimate literary art
or as a means of polemic.

By the beginning of the second century B.C., the
epigram had become the most inclusive and most popular
kind of verse, the main form of lyric poetry,
expressing any incident and any phase of everyday life.
Its popularity continued and was fostered in the
Byzantine world. Almost every Byzantine poet wrote
epigrams; anthologies of ancient and contemporary
examples were created and by the end of the fourth
century A.D. the form was even used in monastic
circles. Early in the seventh century it developed
into a religious poem in iambic trimeter. The elegiac
couplet and hexameter were abandoned, and secular
subjects were no longer popular. Epigrams were
concerned primarily with religious subjects, churches,
icons, religious feasts and holy relics. From the
middle of the seventh to the end of the eight century,
the secular epigram fell into disuse. It was revived
in the ninth century by Theodore (759-826), the abbot
of the Studite monastery, who wrote a series of
epigrams presenting various moods and aspects of
monastic life. He used the form in iambic trimeter to
set forth the duties and privileges of all the members
of the monastic community, from the abbot down to the
door-keeper. Theodore's epigrams established the model
for the secular epigrams that followed. Their meter,
straight manner and simple language were imitated, and
they were copied and widely disseminated. Many
manuscripts of his epigrams still exist.[19] Kassia's
epigrams in simple, direct language are modeled after
Theodore's. They are more appropriately occasional
poems concerned with such diverse subjects as woman,
wealth, stupidity, luck, beauty, the unreliability of
the Armenians and others. She also wrote several
verses describing the monastic life. These are modeled

after Theodore the Studite's verses on the same subject.[20]

Her gnomic verses consist of single-verse, terse, didactic sayings or maxims. Didactic or gnomic verse was very common in Byzantine literature, and except for the epigram, it was the form most widely used and developed throughout the centuries of Byzantine writing. Evidence of gnomic verse can be found in Greek poetry as early as the sixth century B.C., in the works of Pindar. However, the genre did not become popular until the third century B.C. when it was adopted and cultivated by the Hellenistic Greeks of Alexandria as a pedagogical device. At this time the two verse maxim was introduced and became popular, but the single-verse was preferred because it was easy to remember. The Alexandrians favored it as a means of teaching useful information clearly, concisely and attractively in a form that was easy to memorize. Beginning in the third century, they collected and wrote didactic verses on every subject and many of them survived for a long time because of their usefulness as textbooks. The authors most admired and from whose works they copied, adapted or imitated their maxims were Euripides (486-405 B.C.) and Menander (342-291 B.C.). These two authors provided in their works a wealth of concise reflections on human life. The Byzantine writers continued the tradition established by the Alexandrians and wrote didactic verse not to create enduring poetry, but as a teaching and mnemonic device. By the fourth century, didactic verse was not only used to teach subject matter but also for moral teaching. The latter was also very popular in Byzantium, especially with the monastic and ecclesiastical poets. Gregory Nazianzus (329-90 A.D.) produced a work, <u>Gnomic Stanzas</u>, that was widely known and imitated.

In her gnomic verses, Kassia expresses her dislikes and convictions in strong language. Parallels of many of her gnomic verses can be found in writings of earlier authors, both religious and secular,[21] especially Menander, on whose single line verses and topics she seems to have patterned her own. A frequent and favorite theme of Menander was the value of friendship; a large number of Kassia's maxims are

Introduction

concerned with the importance of friendship, and many
echo those found in the Menander collection.[22]
The collection of Kassia's works in this study is
arranged according to the place of each piece in the
ecclesiastical calendar, beginning with September 1,
and the day and service, i. e., vespers or orthos, in
which it is sung. If the hymn is sometimes ascribed to
another author, his name is noted. The study begins
with the hymns of the <u>Menaia</u>, then those in the
<u>Triodion</u>, followed by the canon for the dead and the
secular works, epigrams and gnomic verse. Although it
is almost impossible in a translation to preserve the
exact meter and character of the original, the
translations attempt to give the feeling and meaning of
the works.

Notes

1. The list is reprinted in W. Christ and M. Paranikas, eds., Anthologia Graeca Carminum Christianorum (Leipzig: B. G. Teubner, 1871), p. xli.

2. This is reproduced in Acta Sanctorum, Iunii (Paris and Rome, 1867), p. xvii.

3. A list of Kassia's hymns and discussion of the manuscripts is found in I. Rochow, Studien zu der Person, den Werken und dem Nachleben der Dichterin Kassia (Berlin: Akademie-Verlag, 1967), pp. 35-58.

4. Reprinted in Christ-Paranikas, Anthologia, p. xlix.

5. S. Eustratiades, "Κασιανή ἡ Μελῳδός," Ἐκκλησιαστικός Φάρος, 31 (1932), pp. 97-100.

6. Ibid. p.96.

7. S. Lambros, "Γνῶμαι Κασίας," Δελτίον τῆς Ἱστορικῆς καὶ Ἐθνολογικῆς Ἐταιρείας τῆς Ἑλλάδος, 4 (1982), pp. 533-34; K. Krumbacher, Kasia, Sitzungsberichte der philosophish-philologischen und der historischen Klasse der bayerischen Akademie der Wissenschaften, 3 (1897), pp. 305-70; A. Papadapoulos-Kerameus, "Νέα στιχηρὰ Κασίας μοναχῆ," Byzantinische Zeitschrift, 10 (1901), pp. 60-61; H. J. W. Tillyard, "A Musical Study of the Hymns of Cassia." Byzantinische Zeitschrift, 20 (1911), pp. 419-32; B. A. Mystakides, "Κασία-Κασσιανή, Ὄνομα Αὐτῆς καὶ Γνῶμαι." Ὀρθοδοξία, 1 (1926), pp. 247-51; 314-19; S. Eustratiades, "Κασιανή ἡ Μελῳδός," pp. 92-112.

8. The hymn has been translated into many languages and studied in depth by E. Topping, "The Psalmist, St. Luke and Kassia the Nun," Byzantine Studies, 9 (1932), pp. 199-210.

Introduction

9. H. J. W. Tillyard, "A Musical Study of the Hymns of Cassia," pp. 433-85; J. Raasted, "Voices and Verse in a Troparion of Cassia," _Studies in Eastern Chant_, ed. by M. Velimirovic (London: Oxford University Press, 1973), pp. 171-78; E. Wellesz, _A History of Byzantine Music and Hymnography_ (2nd ed., rev. and enl.; Oxford: Clarendon Press, 1961), pp. 353-54; 395-97.

10. For recent interest in Kassia see, I. Rochow, _Studien...Kassia_, pt.3, pp. 93-190.

11. E.g. P. S. Petrides, "Cassia," _Revue de l'Orient Chretien_, 7 (1902), pp. 235-36; C. A. Trypanis, _Greek Poetry: From Homer to Seferis_, (Chicago: University of Chicago Press, 1981), pp. 435, 445, 447.

12. See note 7.

13. I. Rochow, _Studien...Kassia_, pp. 20-26.

14. The letters of Theodore to Kassia are reprinted in I. Rochow, _Studien...Kassia_, pp. 20-22.

15. A number of poems, novels and theatrical productions have been written based on the legend. See I. Rochow, _Studien...Kassia_, pp. 97-191.

16. W. T. Treadgold, "The Problem of the Marriage of the Emperor Theophilus," _Greek Roman and Byzantine Studies_, 16 (1975), pp. 325-51; "The Bride-Shows of the Byzantine Emperors," _Byzantion_, 49 (1975), pp. 395-413.

17. _Ibid_. p. 413.

18. For a discussion of the history of the bride-shows, see, P. Bourboulis, _Studies in the History of Modern Greek Story-Motives_, (_Hellenika_, Suppl. 2 Thessalonika, 1953).

19. A. Gardner, _Theodore the Studium_ (2nd ed., New York: Lenox Hill, 1974), p.235.

20. Examples of Theodore's epigrams are found in Gardner, p. 245 ff.; for comparison with Kassia's verses on the monastic life see, K. Krumbacher, Kasia, p. 343.

21. K. Krumbacher, Kasia, pp. 341ff.

22. S. Jaekel, Menandri Sententiae (Leipzig: B.G. Teubner, 1964), pp. 33ff.

Introduction

Bibliography

1. Acta Sanctorum, Iunnii. Paris and Rome, 1867.

2. Bankier, J. and D. Lashgari., eds. Women Poets of the World. New York: Macmillan and Co., 1983.

3. Bourboulis, P. P. Studies in the History of Modern Greek Story-Motives. Hellenika, Suppl. 2. Thessalonike, 1953.

4. Brock, S. P. and S. A. Harvey., trans. Holy Women of the Syrian Orient. Berkeley: University of California Press, 1987.

5. Brooks, E. W. "The Marriage of the Emperor Theophilus." Byzantinische Zeitschrift, 10 (1901): 540-45.

6. Bury, J. B. A History of the Eastern Roman Empire from the Fall of Irene to the Accession of Basil (802-67). London: Macmillan and Co., 1912.

7. Charlesworth, J. H., ed. The Old Testament Pseudepigrapha, Vol. 2. New York: Doubleday, 1985.

8. Christ, W. and M. Paranikas. Anthologia Graeca Carminum Christianorum. Leipzig: Teubner, 1871.

9. Eustratiades, S. "Κασιανὴ ἡ Μελωδός." Ἐκκλησιαστικός Φάρος, 31 (1932): 92-112.

10. Gardner, A. Theodore of Studium, His Life and Times. New York: Lenox Hill, 1974.

11. Harvey, S. A. Asceticism and Society in Crisis: John of Ephesus and "The Lives of the Eastern Saints." The Transformation of the Classical Heritage, 18. Berkeley: University of California Press, 1990.

12. Ὡρολόγιον Τὸ Μέγα περιέχον ἅπασαν τὴν ἀνήκουσαν

αὐτῷ ἀκολουθίαν. Athens: Ἀποστολικὴ Διακονία, 1963.

13. Jacobus de Voragine. The Golden Legend. Translated by G. Ryan and H. Ripperger. New York: Arno Press, 1969.

14. Jaekel, S. Menandri Sententias. Leipzig: Teubner, 1964.

15. James, M. R., trans. The Apocryphal New Testament. Oxford: Clarendon Press, 1924.

16. Krumbacher, K. Kasia. Sitzungsberichte der philosophish-phililogischen und der historischen Klasse der bayerischen Akademie der Wissenschaften, III. Munich, 1897.

17. Lampros, S. "Γνῶμαι Κασίας." Δελτίον τῆς ἱστορικῆς καὶ ἐθνολογικῆς ἐταιρείας τῆς Ἑλλάδος, 4 (1892-94): 533-34.

18. Maas, P. "Metrisches zu den Sentenzen der Kassia." Byzantinische Zeitschrift, 10 (1901): 54-59.

19. Μηναῖα τοῦ Ὅλου Ἐνιαυτοῦ, Vol. 1-6. Rome, 1888-1901.

20. Mother Mary and K. Ware., trans. The Festal Menaion. London: Faber and Faber, 1977.

21. _____. The Lenten Triodion. London: Faber and Faber, 1984.

22. Mystakides, B. A. "Κασία-Κασσιανή, Ὅνομα Αὐτῆς καὶ Γνῶμαι." Ὀρθοδοξία, 1 (1926): 247-51; 314-19.

23. Πάντες οἱ βίοι τῶν Ἁγίων. Athens, 1956.

24. Papadapoulos-Kerameus, A. "Νέα στιχηρὰ Κασίας μοναχῆ." Byzantinische Zeitschrift, 10 (1901): 60-61.

25. Petrides, S. "Cassia." Revue de l'Orient

Introduction

Chretien, 7 (1902): 218-44.

26. Politis, N. "Βυζαντιναὶ παραδόσεις, 3: Κασία."
Λαογραφία, 6 (1917): 359-67.

27. Raasted, J. "Voice and Verse in a Troparion of
Cassia." Studies in Eastern Chant. Edited by M.
Velimirovic. London: Oxford University Press, 1973.

28. Rochow, I. Studien zu der Person, den Werken und
dem Nachleben der Dichterin Kassia. Berlin:
Academie-Verlag, 1967.

29. Theodori Studitae Opera Omnia. Migne P. G. 99,
1860.

30. Tillyard, H. J. W. "A Musical Study of the Hymns
of Cassia." Byzantinische Zeitschrift, 20 (1911):
419-85.

31. Topping, E. C. Holy Mothers of Orthodoxy.
Minn.: Light and Life Publishing Co., 1987.

32. Topping, E. C. "The Psalmist, St. Luke and
Kassia the Nun." Byzantine Studies, 9 (1982): 199-
210.

33. Treadgold, W. T. "The Problem of the Marriage of
the Emperor Theophilus." Greek Roman and Byzantine
Studies, 16 (1975): 325-41.

34. _____. "The Bride-Shows of the
Byzantine Emperors." Byzantion, 49 (1979): 395-413.

35. Τριῴδιον Κατανυκτικόν περιέχον ἅπασαν ιὴν
ἀνήκουσαν αὐτῷ ἀκολουθίαν τῆς Ἁγίας καὶ Μεγάλης
Τεσσαρακοστῆς. Athens, 1929.

36. Trypanis, C. A. Greek Poetry: From Homer to
Seferis. Chicago: University of Chicago Press, 1981.

37. Trypanis, C. A. Medieval and Modern Greek
Poetry: An Anthology. Oxford: Clarendon Press, 1951.

38. Turtledove, H., trans. <u>The Chronicle of Theophones</u>. Philadelphia: University of Pennsylvania Press, 1982.

39. Vasiliev, A. A. <u>History of the Byzantine Empire</u>. 2 vols. Madison: University of Wisconsin Press, 1964.

40. Wellesz, E. <u>A History of Byzantine Music and Hymnography</u>. 2nd ed., rev. and enl. Oxford: Clarendon Press, 1961.

Kassia

ΜΕΝΑΙΑ
IDIOMELA

ΜΗΝ ΣΕΠΤΕΜΒΡΙΟΣ
Τῇ Α' ΣΥΜΕΩΝ ΤΟΥ ΣΤΥΛΙΤΟΥ (εἰς τὸν ἑσπερινόν)

I.

Ἐκ ῥίζης ἀγαθῆς
ἀγαθὸς ἐβλάστησε καρπός,
ὁ ἐκ βρέφους ἱερὸς Συμεών,
χάριτι μᾶλλον ἢ γάλακτι τραφείς·
5   καὶ ἐπὶ πέτραν τὸ σῶμα ὑψώσας,
πρὸς Θεὸν δὲ ὑπερυψώσας τὴν διάνοιαν,
αἰθέριον διεδομήσατο ταῖς ἀρεταῖς
ἐνδιαίτημα
καὶ ταῖς θείαις Δυνάμεσι
συμμετεωροπορῶν,
Χριστοῦ γέγονεν οἰκητήριον τοῦ θεοῦ
καὶ Σωτῆρος τῶν ψυχῶν ἡμῶν.

II.

Ἡ τῶν λειψάνων σου θήκη,
Πανεύφημε Πάτερ,
πηγάζει ἰάματα·
καὶ ἡ ἁγία σου ψυχὴ Ἀγγέλοις συνοῦσα,
5   ἀξίως ἀγάλλεται.
Ἔχων οὖν πρὸς Κύριον; Ὅσιε,
παρρησίαν,
καὶ μετὰ τῶν Ἀσωμάτων χορεύων ἐν
οὐρανοῖς,
αὐτὸν ἱκέτευε σωθῆναι τὰς ψυχὰς ἡμῶν.

SEPTEMBER

Simeon the Stylite represents the extremity of Syrian asceticism. He was born in Syria around 386, and adopted the ascetic life at a very young age. In his early monastic career, he spent time in several Syrian monasteries, but his tendency towards severe and eccentric ascetic practices led him into conflict with the monastic establishment. About 412, he mounted a style, a pillar, hence his cognomen, to escape the physical world both spiritually and bodily. There he lived for almost fifty years, mostly in a standing position and without a shelter of any kind, following a rigid schedule of

Symeon the Stylite (September 1)
(at Vespers)

I.

From a good root
a good fruit has grown
Simeon, holy from birth,
you were nourished on grace rather
    than milk;
5   and you lifted your body high upon a
        pillar,
and your thoughts even higher towards
    God,
you lodged on high and lived with the
    virtues,
and walked on air together with the
    Divine Powers.
You became a dwelling place of Christ
    God
and Savior of our souls.

II.

The tomb of your remains,
Oh praiseworthy father,
gushes forth with remedies;
and your holy soul resides with the
    angels,
5   deservedly glorified.
Since you have a special relationship
    with the Lord, Holy One,
and take part with the spiritual
        beings in the heavenly chorus,
beseech him to save our souls.

---

prayer and extreme fasting. He was tended by his
disciples, who brought him the sparse food that he
ate once a week when he was not fasting. His fame as
a holy man was known from Britain to Persia, and
individuals from all levels of society visited him
seeking his advice. It is claimed that he performed
many miracles both in his life and after his death.
The two hymns celebrate his spectacular career.
    The first hymn is credited to Germanos in one
manuscript and anonymous in the Menaion; the second
is attributed to Cyprianos in the Menaion and in most
manuscripts.

4

Menaia

Τῇ ΚΔ' ΘΕΚΛΗΣ ΜΕΓΑΛΟΜΑΡΤΥΡΟΣ (εἰς τὸν ὄρθρον)

Νυμφίον ἔχουσα ἐν οὐρανοῖς Χριστὸν τὸν
    Θεὸν ἡμῶν,
νυμφῶνος κατεφρόνησας τοῦ ἐπιγείου καὶ
    μνηστῆρος,
Θέκλα πρώταθλε
ταῖς γὰρ μητρῴαις θωπείαις ἐμφρόνως μὴ
    πεισθεῖσα,
Παύλῳ ἠκολούθησας,
ἐπ ὤμων ἀραμένη τὸ σημεῖον τοῦ
    Σταυροῦ
καὶ τὸ μὲν πῦρ οὐκ ἐνάρκησας,
τῶν δὲ θηρῶν τὴν ὠμότητα εἰς ἡμερότητα
    μετέβαλες,
φώκας δὲ ἀπενέκρωσας τῇ ἐν Χριστῷ
    καταδύσει
τοῦ ἁγίου Βαπτίσματος.
Ἀλλ' ὡς ἐν ἄθλοις γενναίοις
    διαπρέψασα,
μὴ διαλίπῃς πρεσβεύουσα ἀπαύστως
    τῷ Κυρίῳ
ὑπὲρ τῶν πίστει τελούντων
τὴν ἀεισέβαστον μνήμην σου.

Thekla was eighteen and engaged to be married when she first heard St. Paul preach in her native Iconia, and was immediately converted to Christianity. She rejected her fiance, turned a deaf ear to her mother's pleas and became a follower of Paul. Her mother, angered at her decision, asked the governor of the province to burn her at the stake for lawlessness. When she mounted the pyre and the fire was lit, she made the sign of the cross and the fire was suddenly extinguished by a sudden downpour without touching her. Later, while in Antioch with Paul, she was accused of sacrilege and cast into a stadium with wild beasts. A fierce lioness among them ran to Thekla, lay down at her feet and fought off all the other animals. When the lioness was finally defeated by one of the lions, Thekla saw a large tank of water that was full of seals. She threw herself into it, claiming to baptize herself in the name of Christ. As soon as she entered the water, the seals floated to the top dead. Thekla

Great - martyr Thekla (Sept. 24)
at the Orthos

You rejected the earthly suitor and
bride-chamber,
first among martyrs, Thekla,
and took a heavenly bridegroom, Christ
our God.
You were not persuaded by a mother's
coaxing,
5   but wisely you followed Paul,
and lifted the banner of the Cross on
your shoulders;
Thus the fire did not take hold of
you,
you converted the savagery of the
beasts to gentleness,
you destroyed the seals by your
immersion in Christ
10   as in the Holy Baptism.
Since you were so outstanding in the
noble struggle,
don't neglect to intercede unceasingly
with the Lord
on behalf of those who faithfully
commemorate
your ever-venerable memory.

---

endured many more tortures as she traveled throughout
many cities preaching the Gospel. She died in Iconia
at the age of ninety. The Eastern Church honors her
as the first martyr among women and equal to the
Apostles. This hymn is a precis of her life found in
the apocryphal "Acts of Thekla." It is attributed in
the Menaion and in several manuscripts to Anatolios.

ΜΗΝ ΟΚΤΩΒΡΙΟΣ

Τῇ Η'ΠΕΛΑΓΙΑΣ ΤΗΣ ΟΣΙΑΣ (ἐις τὸν ἐσπερινόν)

Ὅπου ἐπλεόνασεν ἡ ἁμαρτία,
ὑπερεπερίσσευσεν ἡ χάρις,
καθὼς ὁ ᾿Απόστολος διδάσκει
ἐν προσευχαῖς γὰρ καὶ δάκρυσι,
        Πελαγία,

5   τῶν πολλῶν πταισμάτων τὸ πέλαγος
        ἐξήρανας,
κάὶ τὸ τέλος εὐπρόσδεκτον τῷ Κυριῳ διὰ
        τῆς μετανοίας πρασήγαγες·
καὶ νῦν τούτῳ πρεσβεύεις ὑπὲρ τῶν
        ψυχῶν ἡμῶν.

OCTOBER

Pelagia was a notorious courtesan in Antioch, sometime during the late fourth century. One Sunday, against her custom, she went to church and heard a homily given by Bishop Nonnos. She was so moved that she broke into uncontrollable tears and decided to give up her old life and turn to religion and prayer. She begged the bishop to baptize her. A week after her baptism, she disappeared and secretly went to the Mt. of Olives in Jerusalem to live in prayer and strenuous penance in the guise of a man. In Jerusalem she was known as Pelagios the eunuch, a righteous monk who lived a most virtuous life and performed many miracles. Her true identity was not revealed until her death.

The Menaion attributes this hymn to John the Monk; one manuscript claims Theophanes as author and three claim Kassia.

The Pious Pelagia (Oct. 8)
        at Vespers

        Wherever sin has become excessive,
        grace has abounded even more,
        as the Apostle teaches;
        for with tears and prayers, Pelagia,
5   you have dried up the vast sea of
            sins,
        and through penitence brought about
            the result acceptable to the
            Lord;
        and now you intercede with him on
            behalf of our souls.

line 3. The apostle is St. Paul; cf. Romans
        5:20.

ΜΗΝ ΝΟΕΜΒΡΙΟΣ

Τῇ ΙΕ' ΓΟΥΡΙΑ ΣΑΜΩΝΑ ΚΑΙ ΑΒΙΒΟΥ (ἐις τὸν ἑσπερινόν)

'Η "Εδεσσα εὐφραίνεται
ὅτι ἐν τῇ σορῷ τῶν ἁγίων ἐπλουτίσθη,
Γουρία, Σαμωνᾶ καὶ 'Αβίβου'
καὶ τὸ φιλόχριστον ποίμνιον
5 συψχαλουμένη βοᾷ.
Δεῦτε φιλομάρτυρες λαμπρύνθητε
ἐν τῇ μνήμῃ τῇ φαιδρᾷ.
Δεῦτε ὠ φιλέορτοι φωτίσθητε,
ἴδετε φωστῆρας οὐρανίους
10 ἐν ψῇ περιπολεύοντας.
Δεῦτε καὶ ἀκούσατε
οἷον θάνατον πικρὸν
οἱ γενναῖοι ἀδάμαντες ὑπέστησαν
διὰ τὴν ἀτελεύτητον ζωήν.
15 Διὸ καὶ ἐγγυηταὶ ὄντες τῆς ἀληθείας
κορην διέσωσαν ἐν μνήματι ζῶσαν
βεβλημένην.
καὶ τὺν τούτους ἀθετήσυντα παμμίαρον
τῷ ὀλέθρῳ παρέδωκαν
ὡς φονέα καὶ ἀνελεήμονα.
20 καὶ ἐκτενῶς δυσωποῦσι
τὴν παναγίαν Τριάδα,
τοῦ ῥυσθῦναι ἐχ φθορᾶς καὶ πειρασμῶν
καὶ παντοίων κινδύνων
τοὺς ἐν πίστει ἐκτελοῦντας
25 τὰ μνημόσυνα αὐτῶν.

NOVEMBER

Saints Gurias and Samonas were martyred in the persecution under Diocletian in 288, Abibus under Licinius in 316. The hymn discusses a miracle which the saints performed after their martyrdom. A Goth had abducted a maiden whom he found praying with her mother at the tomb of the Saints at Edessa. He then married her and took her to his own country intending to treat her as a slave. His true wife, who was still living, he threw into a tomb alive and let her die. Her friends attempted to do the same thing to the maiden from Edessa. However, the two Saints intervened and miraculously conveyed her back to

Hymn to Saints Gurias, Samonas and Abibus,
Confessors and Martyrs (Nov. 15)
at Vespers

Edessa rejoices
that she has been enriched by the tomb
of the saints;
Gurias, Samonas and Abibus;
and summoning together the Christ-
loving flock,
5   she calls out.
Come, you that love martyrs, rejoice
in their glorious memory.
Come, you that love holy days, be
enlightened;
behold heavenly luminaries
10   walking upon the earth.
Come and hear
what kind of bitter death
these unconquerable brave men
underwent
for everlasting life.
15   Whereby, being sureties for the truth
they save the maiden who had been
thrown alive in the tomb.
And the all-abominable one who behaved
despicably
they committed to destruction
as murderer and unmerciful.
20   And zealously they implore
the All-Holy Trinity
to save from ruin and temptation
and all manner of danger
those who in faith keep
25   their memorial rite.

Edessa. Later, when the Goth revisited the city,
they miraculously revealed his crime and caused him
to be punished.

Τῇ ΙΣΤ΄ ΜΑΤΘΑΙΟΥ ΤΟΥ ΕΥΑΓΓΕΛΙΣΤΟΥ (εἰς τὸν ἑσπερινόν)

I.   Ἐκ πυθμένος κακίας ἐσχάτης
         πρὸς ἀκρότατον ὕψος ἀρετῆς,
         ὡς ἀετὸς ὑψιπέτης,
         παραδόξως ἀνέδραμες, Ματθαῖε
             πανεύφημε·
5   τοῦ γὰρ χκαλύψαντος οὐρανοὺς ἀρετῇ,
         καὶ τῆς συνέσεως αὐτοῦ πᾶσαν τὴν γῆν
             πληρώσαντος,
         Χριστοῦ ἀκολουθήσας τοῖς ἴχνεσι,
         μιμητὴς διάπυρος ἐν πᾶσιν αὐτοῦ
             πεφανέρωσαι,
         εὐαγγελιζόμενος εἰρήνην, ζωὴν καὶ
             σωτηρίαν,
10   τοῖς πειθαρχοῦσιν εὐσεβῶς τοῖς θείοις
             προστάγμασιν·
         ἐν οἷς ἡμᾶς καθοδήγησον, εὐαρεστοῦντας
             τῷ Κτίστῃ,
         καὶ σὲ μακαρίζοντας.

II.   εἰς τὸν ὄρθον

         Κροτήσωμεν ἐν ᾄσμασι σήμερον, πιστοί,
         ἐπὶ τῇ μνήμῃ τοῦ σεπτοῦ Ἀποστόλου,
         καὶ Εὐαγγελιστοῦ Ματθαίου οὗτος γὰρ
         ρίψας τὸν ζυγόν, καὶ τὸν χρυσὸν τοῦ
             τελωνίου,
         ἠκολούθησε Χριστῷ, καὶ κήρυξ τοῦ
             Εὐαγγελίου
5   θεῖος ἐχρημάτισεν
         ὅθεν ἐξῆλθε προφητικῶς ὁ φθόγγος αὐτοῦ
         εἰς τὴν οἰκουμένην,
         καὶ πρεσβεύει σωθῆναι τὰς ψυχὰς ἡμῶν.

_____

Before becoming a disciple, Matthew was a
publican, a tax collector, not a well-thought-of
occupation. As a disciple he was the first to bring
the message of God to the world. At the time of the
hymn's composition, Matthew was thought to be the
first of the gospel writers. He begins his gospel by
tracing the human descent of Christ and is the one to
stress, more than the other Evangelists, Christ's
human genealogy. Thus he is often portrayed with the

Matthew the Evangelist (Nov. 16)
at Vespers

I.
From the depths of evil
to the extreme height of goodness,
soaring like an eagle,
you rose incredibly quickly, all
    praising Matthew;

5
covering the skies with excellence,
and filling all the earth with your
    knowledge,
you followed in the footsteps of
    Christ,
proving to be an ardent imitator of
    Him in all things,
preaching peace, life and salvation

10
for those who reverently observe the
    divine commands
by which you guide us to be agreeable
    to the Creator,
and we bless you.

II.
at the Orthos

Faithful, today let us applaud with
    hymn,
in remembrance of the holy Apostle,
and Evangelist Matthew; for he threw
    off the yoke and the gold of the
    publican,
and followed Christ, and as herald of
    the Gospel

5
had dealings only with the divine;
from where his utterance came
    prophetically
to the inhabited world,
and he intercedes to save our souls.

---

symbol of a winged man, the first of the winged
creatures mentioned in Ezekial (1:5-6) and in
Revelation (4:6-9), which signify Christ's human
nature. The hymn discusses Matthew's rise from
publican to herald of the Gospel. Three manuscripts
attribute the hymn to Byzantios. In the Menaion and
several manuscripts it appears without an author.

Gramley Library
Salem College
Winston-Salem, NC 27108

ΜΗΝ ΔΕΚΕΜΒΡΙΟΣ

Τῇ Α΄ ΒΑΡΒΑΡΑ ΜΑΡΤΥΡΟΣ (ἐις τὸν ὄρθον)

Ἠσχύνθη ὁ Βάσκανος ἐχθρὸς
ὑπὸ γυναικὸς ἡττώμενος,
ὅτι τὴν Προμήτορα ἔσχεν ὄργανον πρὸς
    ἁμαρτίαν·
ὁ γὰρ ἐκ Παρθένου σαρκωθεὶς
5   Λόγος τοῦ Πατρός,
ἀτρέπτως καὶ ἀφύρτως,
ὡς οἶδε μόνος αὐτός,
τὴν κατάραν ἔλυσε τῆς Εὔας καὶ τοῦ
    Ἀδάμ,
Χριστὸς ὁ στεφανώσας ἀξίως, Βαρβάραν
    τὴν Μάρτυρα,
10   καὶ δἰ αὐτῆς δωρούμενος τῷ κόσμῳ
    ἱλασμὸν καὶ τὸ μέγα ἔλεος.

DECEMBER

This hymn not only extols St. Barbara's martyrdom but espouses the view that women have aided in man's redemption, beginning with the Virgin Mary. She bore Christ, whose incarnation brought about the regeneration of man; Barbara is an instrument for man's atonement. This view reflects Kassia's answer to the Emperor Theophilos (see above, Life and Times of the Author).

St. Barbara is one of the better known and much supplicated saints of the Eastern Church. She is venerated for her unwavering faith in the presence of the harshest and most inhumane tortures, ordered by her own father. For this, Christ rewarded her with the victor's crown of martyrdom and a blessed afterlife.

The hymn is attributed to Byzantios in the Menaion. One manuscript claims Cyprianos as author, and another Anatolios.

The Great-martyr Barbara (Dec. 4)
at the Orthos

The evil one has been dishonored,
defeated by a woman,
because he held the First-Mother
as an instrument of sin;
5   for the Logos of the Father,
simple and immutable,
as only he is known,
was made flesh of a Virgin
and removed the curse of Eve and Adam,
10   Christ deservedly crowned Barbara the
Martyr,
and through her gives to the world a
means of atonement and great
mercy.

lines 1-9. The Virgin Mary, by giving birth to
Christ, defeated the evil serpent who tempted
Eve.

I. Τῇ ΙΓ' ΕΥΣΤΡΑΤΙΟΥ, ΑΥΞΕΝΤΙΟΥ καὶ λοιπῶν (ἐις τὸν
   ὄρθον)

Τὴν πεντάχορδον λύραν,
καὶ πεντάφωτον λυχνίαν,
τῆς τοῦ Θεοῦ ἐκκλησίας
τοὺς θεοφόρους μάρτυρας
5   φερωνύμως τιμήσωμεν
καὶ εὐσεβῶς ἐγκωμιάσωμεν.
Χαίροις, ὁ χαλῶς ὑπὸ Θεοῦ στρατευθεὶς
ἐν τῇ ἐπουρανίῳ στρατείᾳ,
καὶ τῷ στρατολογήσαντι ἀρέσας,
10   ὁ ἐν ῥήτορσι ῥήτωρ,
Εὐστράτις θεόσοφε.
Χαίροις, ὁ τὸ τάλαντον τὸ ἐκ Θεοῦ σοι
       πιστευθὲν
ἐπαυξήσας εἰς πλῆθος,
Αὐξέντιε μακάριε.
15   Χαίροις, ὁ τερπνότατος ὅρπηξ
τῆς θεϊκῆς εὐγενείας,
Εὐγένιε θεόφρον.
Χαίροις, ὁ ὡραῖος τῇ μορφῇ,
τῇ δὲ γνώμῃ ὑπέρλαμπρος
20   καὶ ἀμφοτεροδέξιος,
ὁ ἐν τοῖς θείοις ὅρεσιν ἐνδιαιτώμενος
       ὅλως,
πανόλβιε Ὀρέστα.
Χαίροις, ὁ στίλβων καὶ διαυγὴς
       μαργαρίτης,
ὁ τὰς βασάνους τὰς πικρὰς
25   χαρμονίκως ὑπομείνας,
Μαρδάριε ἀήττητε.
Χαίροις, ὁ ἰσάριθους χορὸς τῶν
       φρονίμων παρθένων.
Οὓς χαθιχετεύσωμεν
πάσης ὀργῆς καὶ θλίψεως λυτρώσασθαι
30   καὶ τῆς ἀφράστου αὐτῶν δόξης
συμμετόχους ποιῆσαι
τοὺς τὴν ἐτήσιον αὐτῶν
μνήμῃ γεραίροντας.

St. Eustratius and His Fellow-Martyrs (Dec. 13)
at the Orthos

I.

                    The five-stringed lute,
                    and five-fold lamp,
                    of God's Church,
                    the divinely inspired martyrs
    5   so suitably named, let us honor
                    and reverently praise.
                    Hail, you who nobly served under God
                    in the heavenly expedition
                    and were pleasing to the Leader,
    10   orator among orators,
                    Eustratius, wise in the things of God.
                    Hail, you who increased in quantity
                    the talent entrusted to you from God
                    blessed Auxentius
    15   Hail, you who are the most pleasing
                        descendent
                    of divine nobility,
                    godly-minded Eugenius.
                    Hail, you who are fair in form,
                    exceedingly distinguished in judgment
    20   and always ready,
                    who lives forever on the mountains of
                        God,
                    truly blessed Orestes
                    Hail, shining and radiant pearl,
                    who endured the bitter tortures
    25   quietly,
                    unconquered Mardarius.
                    Hail, evenly-balanced chorus of wise
                        virgins.
                    Let us entreat them
                    to deliver from all wrath and
                        oppression
    30   and make partakers
                    of their ineffable glory
                    those who celebrate
                    their yearly feast.

lines 12-13. The reference is to the Parable of the
    Talents (Matt. 25:14-30) and Jesus' teaching
    that each person should make the most of his
    God-given talents or abilities.

II.

εἰς τὸν ὄρθον

Ὑπὲρ τῶν Ἑλλήνων παιδείαν
τὴν τῶν ἀποστόλων σοφίαν προέκριναν οἱ
    ἅγιοι μάρτυρες,
τὰς βίβλους τῶν ῥητόρων καταλείψαντες
καὶ ταῖς τῶν ἁλιέων διαπρέψαντες.
5 Ἐκεῖ μὲν γὰρ, εὐγλωττίαν ῥημάτων,
ἐν δὲ ταῖς τῶν ἀγραμμάτων θεηγορίαις
τὴν τῆς Τριάδος ἐδιδάσκοντο
    θεογνωσίαν,
ἐν ᾗ πρεσβεύουσιν ἐν εἰρήνῃ φυλαχθῆναι
τὰς ψυχὰς ἡμῶν.

_____

        In these hymns Eustratius, Auxentios, Eugenius,
Orestes and Mardarius are all commemorated. They all
were born in Cappodocia, all were well to do and
well-versed in the teachings of classical antiquity.
Eustratius in particular, was an accomplished orator,
served as an officer in the Roman army and was an
archivist for the province of Nicopolis in Asia
Minor. During the reign of Diocletian (285-313), all
openly professed and freely preached the Christian
faith for which they suffered many, diverse tortures.
Auxentius, Eugenius and Mardarius died while being
tortured; Eustratius and Orestes survived the
tortures and were sent to Sebaste, where they were
put to death by fire in 296. The first hymn gives a
biographical sketch of each martyr; the second
celebrates their preference for the teachings of the
fishermen, the disciples of Christ, over those of the
ancient Greeks.

line 27. ἰσάριθμος - evenly balanced, a term used of
          the five wise virgins by Methodius, Bishop of
          Olympius (c.311) in his exegesis of the
          Parable of the Ten Virgins (Matt. 25:1-13).
          These virgins are described as 'evenly-balanced'
          because they were vigilant to keep all of their
          senses pure, and thus were able to join in
          fellowship with Jesus. See Methodius' Symposium
          6:3. The poet is comparing the five martyrs to
          the five wise virgins.

II.
                        at the Orthos

                Above the teachings of the Greeks
                the holy martyrs preferred the wisdom
                    of the apostles,
                abandoning the books of the orators
                and excelling in those of the
                    fishermen.
       5   For there indeed was the eloquence of
                    words,
                and in the preaching of the uneducated
                they learned the divine knowledge of
                    the Trinity,
                by which they serve as envoys that our
                    souls be guarded in peace.

Τῇ ΚΕ΄ Η ΓΕΝΝΗΣΙΣ ΤΟΥ ΣΩΤΗΡΟΣ (εἰς τὸν ἑσπερινόν)

        Αὐγούστου μοναρχήσαντος ἐπὶ τῆς γῆς
        ἡ πολυαρχία τῶν ἀνθρώπων ἐπαύσατο
        καὶ σοῦ ἐνανθρωπήσαντος ἐκ τῆς ἁγνῆς
        ἡ πολυθεΐα τῶν εἰδώλων κατήργηται
5   ὑπὸ μίαν βασιλείαν ἐγκόσμιον
        αἱ πόλεις γεγένηται·
        καὶ εἰς μίαν δεσποτείαν θεότητος
        τὰ ἔθνη ἐπίστευσαν
        ἀπεγράφησαν οἱ λαοί, τῷ δόγματι τοῦ
          Καίσαρος
10   ἐπεγράφημεν οἱ πιστοί, ὀνόματι
          θεότητος
        σοῦ τοῦ ἐνανθρωπήσαντος θεοῦ ἡμῶν
        μέγα σου τὸ ἔλεος, Κύριε, δόξα σοι.

This is considered one of Kassia's more noteworthy troparia after the famous hymn on Mary Magdelene. In concise, simple language it glorifies the new-born king, Christ. Using several pairs of ideas in opposition, the hymn contrasts the rule of the first Roman Emperor Augustus (27 B.C. - A.D.14), who established the Pax Romana with that of the reign of Christ, and emphasizes the supremacy and omnipotence of His reign. The contrast is further stressed by the use of the aorist and perfect tense.

The Birth of Christ (December 25)
at Vespers

When Augustus reigned alone upon the
    earth,
the many Kingdoms of men came to an
    end;
and since You were made man of a pure
    Virgin
the many gods of idols have been
    destroyed
5 The cities have come
under one universal Kingdom
and the nations came to believe
in one divine dominion.
The people were registered by the
    decree of Caesar;
10 we, the faithful, have been inscribed
    in the name of
Your divinity when You our God were
    made man.
Great is Your mercy, Lord; glory to
    You.

line 2. ἐπαύσατο, "came to an end," the aorist tense
denoting a single occurrence in past time.

line 4. κατήργηται, "have been destroyed," perfect
tense denoting a continuing accomplished
situation. All other divinities have been
destroyed once and for all.

I.

'Ως ὡράθης, Χριστέ,
ἐν Βηθλεὲμ τῆς 'Ιουδαίας
ἐκ Παρθένου τικτόμενος
καὶ τοῖς σπαργάνοις ὥσπερ νήπιον
        ἐνειλούμενος
5   καὶ ἐν φάτνῃ ἀνακλινόμενος
δῆμος ἀγγέλων ἐξ ὕψους ἐδόξαζε
τὴν πολλήν σου πρὸς ἀνθρώπους
        οἰκονομίαν
ὁ διὰ σπλάγχνα οἰκτιρμῶν
σάρκα περιβαλλόμενος
10   καὶ τὸ πρόσλημμα θεώσας
τῶν βροτῶν, Κύριε, δόξα σοι.

II.

'Ως ὡράθης, Χριστέ,
ἐκ γυναικὸς σεσαρκωμένος
κατεπλήττετο τὴν σὴν
συγκατάβασιν ἡ δὲ τεκοῦσα
5   καὶ δακρύουσα, σῶτερ, ἔλεγε·
πῶς σε βρέφος φέρω τὸν ἄχρονον
γάλακτι δέ σε πῶς τρέφω τὸν τρέφοντα
πᾶσαν κτίσιν θεϊκῇ σου τῇ δυναστείᾳ;
'Ο διὰ σπλάγχνα οἰκτιρμῶν
10   σάρκα περιβαλλόμενος
καὶ τὸ πρόσλημμα θεώσας
τῶν βροτῶν, Κύριε, δόξα σοι.

The following eight hymns on the birth of Christ
do not appear in the **Menaion** or any other official
liturgical book. They are found in only two
manuscripts in the library of Mt. Athos, and were
discovered and transcribed by St. Eustratiades,
"Κασιανὴ ἡ Μελῳδός," Ἐκκλησιαστικὸς Φάρος, 31
(1932), pp. 102-05. The phraseology of these hymns
is similar to that of the hymns found in the official
liturgical books and sung on that day. All emphasize
and glorify Jesus' paradoxical union of the human and
the divine and his great compassion and
condenscension for mankind. Kassia's hymns stress
Christ's extreme humility more than the other hymns.
Every one of her hymns seems to emphasize the poverty
that Jesus assumed at his birth.

I.

at Vespers

When you appeared, Christ,
in Bethlehem of Judea
born from a Virgin
and wrapped in swaddling clothes as a
    new-born
5   and lying in a manger,
a company of angels from on high
    praised
your great concession towards mankind
who through the deepest compassion
put on a body
10   and deified the mortal being;
glory to you, Lord.

II.

When you appeared, Christ,
made flesh from a woman
she who bore you,
astounded by your condescension,
5   tearfully said, savior;
how can I bear you as infant who are
    eternal
how can I nourish with milk you who
    nourish
the whole of creation with your divine
    power?
who through the deepest compassion
10   put on a body
and deified the mortal body
glory to you, Lord.

III.

           Ὡς ὡράθης, σωσήρ,
           ὁ βασιλεύων τῶν αἰώνων
           ὑπὸ μάγων προσκυνούμενος
           ὁδηγηθέντων δι' ἀστέρος σοι, δόξης
             ἥλιε,
5   τὴν πτωχείαν σου κατεπλήττοντο
           καὶ χρυσὸν δὲ καὶ σμύρναν καὶ λίβανον
           σοὶ προσῆξαν ἐπὶ φάτνης ἀνακειμένῳ
           ὁ διὰ σπλάγχνα οἰκτιρμῶν
           σάρκα περιβαλλόμενος
10   καὶ τὸ πρόσλημμα θεώσας
           τῶν βροτῶν, Κύριε, δόξα σοι.

IV.

           Ὡς ὡράθης, Χριστέ,
           ἐπὶ τῆς ἐπιδημήσας
           καὶ πτωχεύσας τὸ ἀλλότριον
           πᾶσα ἡ κτίσις ὡς δεσπότῃ σοι
             προσεκόμιζε
5   χαριστήριον χαίρουσα ὕμνον
           ἄνθροποι τὴν τεκοῦσάν σε,
           ἡ γῆ τὸ σπήλαιον καὶ οἱ μάγοι τὰ δῶρα
           ὁ διὰ σπλάγχνα οἰκτιρμῶν
           σάρκα περιβαλλόμενος
10   καὶ τὸ πρόσλημμα θεώσας
           τῶν βροτῶν, Κύριε, δόξα σοι.

V.

           Ἄγγελοι ἐν σπηλαίῳ
           ἐπιστάντες ὕμνουν σε, Κύριε,
           τεχθέντα ἐκ Παρθένου ὡς ἄνθρωπον
           μάγοι δὲ καὶ ποιμένες
5   σὺν αὐτοῖς, Χριστέ, προσεκύνουν σε
           ἐν φάτνῃ ἀνακείμενον νήπιον·
           οἱ μὲν καταπλαγέντες
           τὲν πτωχείαν σου, Λόγε, τὴν ξένην,
           οἱ δὲ δῶρα χρυσόν σοι
10   κομίζοντες καὶ σμύρναν καὶ λιβανον
           μεθ' ὧν βοῶμέν σοι,
           εὐεργέτα τῶν ἀπάντων
           Κύριε, δόξα σοι.

III.

> When you appeared, Savior,
> who reigns through the ages,
> you were worshipped by the Magi
> having been led by a star to you, sun
>   of glory;
5   they were astounded by your poverty
> and offered to you lying in a manger,
> gold, frankincense and myrrh
> who through the deepest compassion
> put on a body
> and deified the mortal being;
10   glory to you, Lord.

IV.

> When you appeared, Christ,
> to live among the people on earth
> becoming poor, to the contrary
> the whole creation added adornments to
>   you as lord
5   the people rejoicing offered a hymn of
>   thanksgiving
> to the one who bore you;
> the earth offered the cave and the
>   Magi the gifts;
> to you who through the deepest
> compassion put on a body
10   and deified the mortal being;
> glory to you, Lord.

V.

> Angels present at the cave
> sang hymns of praise to you, Lord,
> born from a virgin as a man;
> Magi and shepherds with them
5   worshipped you, Christ,
> lying in a manger, newborn;
> some were impressed by
> your unusual poverty, O Logos;
> others carried gifts to you,
10   gold and myrrh and frankincense,
> joining them we cry aloud to you,
> benefactor of all,
> glory to you, Lord.

VI.

Τὸν ἥλιον τῆς δόξης
φωτεινῆς σου μήτρας ἀνίσχουσα,
ὦ κεχαριτωμένη πανάμωμε,
τοῖς ἐν σκότει τοῦ βίου
5   ταῖς ἀκτῖσι θελήσαντα ὑφαπλῶσαι
λάμψιν σωτήριον
παρθένος μετὰ τόκον
ὡς πρὸ τόκου μένεις ὑπὲρ λόγον
καὶ τοῦτον τοῖς σπαργάνοις
10   ὡς νέφεσι καλύπτεις φωτίζοντα
τοὺς πίστει κράζοντας,
εὐεργέτα τῶν ἁπάντων
Κύριε, δόξα σοι.

VII.

Ἡ κτίσις ἐφωτίσθη
ἐπὶ γῆς τεχθέντος σου, δέσποτα,
καὶ οὐρανοί σε φόβῳ ἀνύμνησαν
ποιμένες μετὰ μάγων
5   εὐσεβῶς σε ἐδόξαζον
ὡς κατεῖδόν σε, Λόγε, πτωχεύσαντα
καὶ σπάργανα φοροῦντα
δι' ὧν πάντων ἔλυσας, οἰκτίρμον,
σειρὰς τῶν ἐγκλημάτων
10   συνδήσας ἀφθαρσίᾳ ἡμῶν τὴν ζωὴν
τῶν βοώντων σοι
εὐεργέτα τῶν ἁπάντων
Κύριε, δόξα σοι.

VI.

> The sun of glory
> came forth from your radiant womb,
> oh highly favored all-blameless,
> ordained to spread with its rays
> 5   the light of salvation;
> you remained a virgin after the birth
> as you were before it,
> something unexplainable;
> and you covered him with swaddling
>   clothes
> 10   as a cloud, he who enlightens
> those who cry out with faith,
> benefactor of all,
> glory to you, Lord.

VII.

> Creation was enlightened
> by your birth on earth, Lord,
> and the heavens praised you with fear
> shepherds along with Magi
> 5   reverently glorified you
> when they saw you, O Logos, being poor
> and wearing swaddling clothes
> through which, merciful one, you broke
> all bands of sin
> 10   uniting life with immortality
> for those who entreat you,
> benefactor of all,
> glory to you, Lord.

lines 7-11. Christ's coming to earth as a humble
    man, symbolized by the swaddling clothes, freed
    mankind from all transgressions and made it
    possible for him to attain immortality through
    faith in Him.

VIII.

Σήμερον σαρκοῦται Θεὸς
'εκ Παρθένου ἀγίας
καὶ πτωχεύει Κύριος
ἵνα πλουτήσῃ πτωχείαν
5   ἣν ἐταπείνωσεν ὁ ὄφις·
νῦν προσέλθωμεν πρὸς αὐτὸν
καὶ φωτισθῶμεν
ἐξανέτειλε γὰρ φῶς τοῖς ἐσκοτισμένοις
καὶ ταπεινοὺς ὕψωσε
10   τοὺς ἀγγελικῶς μελῳδοῦντας
δόξα ἐν ὑψίστοις Θεῷ
καὶ ἐπὶ γῆς εἰρήνη
ἐν ἀνθρώποις εὐδοκία.

VIII.

<pre>
              Today God is made flesh
              by a holy Virgin
              and the Lord becomes poor
              so that poverty might be made rich
  5   which the serpent had debased;
              now let us approach him
              and be enlightened
              for the light has shone upon those in
                  darkness
              and exalted the humble,
 10   those who like the angels sing
              glory to God in the highest
              and on earth peace
              with good will among men.
</pre>

ΜΗΝ ΙΑΝΟΥΑΡΙΟΣ

Τῇ Α' ΒΑΣΙΛΕΙΟΥ ΤΟΥ ΜΕΓΑΛΟΥ (ἐις τὸν ἐσπερινόν)

Πάντων τῶν ᾿Αγίων ἀνεμάξω τὰς ἀρετὰς,
Πατὴρ ἡμῶν Βασίλειε·
Μωυσέως τὸ πρᾶον,
᾿Ηλιοῦ τὸν ζῆλον,
5   Πέτρου τὴν ὁμολογίαν,
᾿Ιωάννου τὴν Θεολογίαν,
ὡς Παῦλος ἐκβοῶν οὐκ ἐπαύσω·
Τίς ἀσθενεῖ, καὶ οὐκ ἀσθενῶ;
τίς σχανδαλίζεται, καὶ οὐκ ἐγὼ
πυροῦμαι;
10   ῞Οθεν σὺν αὐτοῖς αὐλιζόμενος,
ἱκέτευε σωθῆναι τὰς ψυχὰς ἡμῶν.

JANUARY

St. Basil is considered one of the luminaries of
the Eastern Church, one of the three great
Cappadocian Fathers who are known as the "three
hierarchs." The other two include Gregory Nazianzus,
a close friend of Basil's, and Basil's younger
brother, Gregory of Nyssa. Basil studied in the best
rhetorical schools of Athens and Constantinople,
preparing for the profession of rhetor, but was
somewhat reluctantly ordained to the priesthood by
Eusebius of Caesarea. Once ordained, he proved
himself to be an exemplary churchman, both as a
monastic leader and as a bishop of the Church. A
gentle and humble person, but with great courage and
conviction, he devoted his life to the people of his
diocese, to the poor and to the defense of orthodox
Christianity against the Arian heresy. He is
credited with establishing a welfare and social
service program in his diocese of Caesarea. His
works include over three hundred letters dealing with
matters of dogma, numerous homilies, several books
and a divine liturgy performed ten times during the
year on special days. His writings and outlook show
the fusion of Christianity with classical culture,
marking him as a true Christian humanist. Because of
his great wisdom, his scholarly writings, his efforts
on behalf of those in need and his ardent promotion

Basil the Great (Jan. 1)
at Vespers

Our Father Basil,
you assumed the virtues of all saints;
the gentleness of Moses,
the zeal of Elias,
5   the concession of Peter,
the divine teachings of John;
like Paul you cried out, "I will not
    rest;
Who is weak, and I'm not weak?
Who falls into sin and I'm not
    burning?"
10   From your dwelling place with the
    saints,
entreat to save our souls.

lines 7-9.   2 Cor. 11:29.

---

and defense of orthodoxy, he is called Great.   The
Church honors his memory each year on the day on
which he died, January 1, A.D. 379.   This hymn
celebrates Basil's many virtues.   Several manuscripts
and the Menaion attribute it to Basil the Monk, a
minor religious poet of the tenth century.

Τῇ Β' ΠΡΟΕΟΡΤΙΑ ΤΩΝ ΦΩΤΩΝ (εἰς τὸν ἑσπερινόν)

I.

　　　　"Ως ὡράθης, Χριστέ,
　　　　μετὰ τῶν δούλων ὁ δεσπότης
　　　　πρὸς τὰ ρεῖθρα τοῦ Ἰορδάνου ἑρχόμενος
　　　　καὶ παρὰ δούλου τοῦ Προδρόμου σου
　　　　χειραπτούμενος
5　　　καὶ τῷ ὕδατι βαπτιζόμενος
　　　　τάξεις ἀγγέλων ἑξίσταντο βλέπουσαι
　　　　τὴν πολλήν σου συγκατάβασιν, εὐεργέτα,
　　　　ὁ βαπτισθῆναι δι' ἡμᾶς
　　　　σαρκὶ καταδεξάμενος
10　　καὶ τοὺς σπίλους ἀποσμίξας
　　　　τῶν βροτῶν, Κύριε, δόξα σοι.

────────────────

　　These three hymns are found in only one
manuscript, Cod. Paris 13, and are attributed to
Kassia. The manuscript lists them as hymns of the
forefeast of the Theophany or Epiphany celebrated on
January 5, not January 2, as stated. However, they
belong to the feast day of John the Baptist
celebrated on January 7. Their theme and phraseology
is similar to that of the official hymns in the
Menaion sung on that day. A transcription of the
hymns is found in S. Eustratiades, "Κασιανή ἡ
Μελωδός," pp. 106-10.

Forefeast of the Theophany (Jan. 2)
at Vespers

I.

When you appeared, Christ,
the lord among the servants
approaching the waters of Jordan
and touched by the hand of your
    servant, the Forerunner
5   and baptized in the waters,
the host of angels were amazed seeing
your great condescension, benefactor,
who was baptized for us,
accepted a human body
10 and wiped clean the sins
of the mortals; glory to you, Lord.

II.

'Ιησοῦς ὁ Χριστὸς
ὁ φωτισμὸς τῶν ἐν τῷ σκότει
τὴν ἀνάπλασιν ἡμῶν ἐργαζόμενος
πρὸς 'Ιωάννεν παρεγένετο ἐξαιτούμενος
5   βαπτισθῆναι ἀναβοῶν αὐτῷ
λοῦσόν με τούτοις τοῖς ὕδασι θέλοντα
ἐν αὐτοῖς ἀναχωνεῦσαι φύσιν ἀνθρώπων
παλαιωθεῖσαν τῇ φθορᾷ
ὅλην τε τῇ τοῦ ὄφεως
10   δουλωθεῖσαν πανουργίᾳ
δυσσεβῶς, Κύριε, δόξα σοι.

III.

Πῶς σε πῦρ χόρτος ὤν,
ὦ ποιητά χειροθετήσω;
πῶς ροαί σε ποταμοῦ ὑποδέξονται
πέλαγος μέγα τῆς θεότετος χρηματίζοντα
5   καὶ πηγὴν ζωῆς ἀδαπάνητον;
πῶς σε βαπτίσω τὸν ῥύπον μὴ ἔχοντα
τὸν δὲ σπίλον τῶν ἀνθρώπων
        προσαφαιροῦντα
τῷ δι' ἡμᾶς ἐκ τῆς ἁγνῆς
--ἔφη ὁ ἐκ τῆς στείρας τεχθεὶς--
10   ἐγὼ χρείαν ἔχω τοῦ σοῦ
βαπτισμοῦ, Κύριε, δόξα σοι.

II.

Jesus the Christ
who enlightens those in darkness,
who brings about our spiritual
renewal, came to John asking
5   to be baptized, calling out to him:
wash me with these waters; with them
I shall regenerate
the whole of mankind
that is ensconced in corruption
10   and impiously enslaved by the
        serpent's
cunning, glory to you, Lord.

III.

Oh creator, how shall I lay my hands
        upon you;
who are the divine fire?
How will the waters of the river
        receive you
who are regarded as a great sea of
        divinity
5   and the inexhaustible source of life?
How shall I baptize you who are not
        polluted
and who moreover takes away the sin of
        mankind
for which on our account you were born
        of a virgin,
said he who was born of a barren woman
10   I have need of your baptism.
Glory to you, Lord.

Τῇ Ι΄ ΓΡΗΓΟΡΙΟΥ ΝΥΣΣΗΣ (ἐις τὸν ἑσπερινόν)

Τὸν τῆς σοφίας λόγον σου καταγλαίσας
    ἐν ἀρετῇ ἀπροσίτῳ,
περικαλλὴς ἀμφοτέρωθεν γέγονας,
    Νυσσαέων Γρεγόριε,
ἐν τῇ θεοφθόγγῳ σου φωνῇ
ὡραίζων καὶ τέρπων τὸν λαὸν γνωστικῶς,
Τριάδος τὸ ὁμόθεον πανσόφως
    ἐχτιθέμενος
ὅθεν καὶ ἐν ὀρθοδόξοις δόγμασι
τὰς ἀλλοφύλους αἱρέσεις ἐκπολεμήσας,
τὸ κράτος τὸ τῆς Πίστεως
ἐν τοῖς πέρασιν ἤγειρας.
Χριστῷ παριστάμενος σὸν τοῖς ἀΰλοις
    Λειτουργοῖς,
ταῖς ψυχαῖς ἡμῶν αἴτησαι
εἰρήνην καὶ τὸ μέγα ἔλεος.

5

10

Gregory of Nyssa was the younger brother of
Basil the Great, the third member of the "three
hierarchs" (see above, Jan. 1), and the most profound
thinker of the three. The hymn praises Gregory's
clarifying statement of the relationship of the three
persons of the Trinity. It was his concept of
"coinherence" that helped to give the doctrine of the
Trinity its final form and has remained the formula
in the theology of the Eastern Church. The one
Godhead undivided and unchanging exists
simultaneously in three persons or modes of being.
Most manuscripts attribute the hymn to Anatolios; the
Menaion lists it anonymously.

Gregory of Nyssa (Jan. 10)
     at Vespers

You glorified your wise words with
     unmatched virtue,
excelling in both, Gregory of Nyssa,
with your God-inspired statement
you spiritually enlightened and gave
     joy to the people
5   most clearly setting forth the
          identity of the nature of the
          Trinity
     with which along with the orthodox
          tenets
     you defeated the foreign heresies,
     and established the authority of Faith
     to the ends of the earth.
10   Since you serve Christ along with the
          angels,
     request for our souls
     peace and great mercy.

Τῇ Κ' ΕΥΘΥΜΙΟΥ ΤΟΥ ΜΕΓΑΛΟΥ (ἐις τὸν ἐσπερινόν)

Εὐθυμεῖτε, ἔλεγε τοῖς γεννήτορσιν
   Ἄγγελος Κυρίου,
ὅτι παιδίον ἐκ σπλάγχνων γεννήσεται
   ὑμῖν,
εὐθυμίας φερώνυμον
ἐνεφύης δὲ γαστρὶ φέρων αὐτοῖς τὸ
   ἐπάγγελμα
5   καὶ ἐκ σπαργάνων τῇ εὐχῇ
συνανετράφης, Πάτερ Εὐθύμιε.

The hymn is a paronomasia, a play on the word
"euthemeo," to be of good cheer or to be content.
St. Euthemius was born in 377 to a couple who longed
for children but were unable to bear any. Because of
their great joy and happiness at his birth, they
named him Euthemius, "of good cheer." Euthemius
studied under the bishop of Melitene, Eutroius, who
ordained him into the priesthood at a very early age.
After his ordination, he traveled to Palestine and
founded many monasteries, both laura, isolated
hermitages and coenobia, monastic communities where
monks live and work together. He himself preferred a
more solitary life. It was Euthemius who established
the direction of Palestinian monasticism, and for
this the Church honors him as one of its more
important ascetics. He died on January 20, 473, at
the age of 96. His life was written by Cyril of
Scythopolis, a notable hagiographer of the sixth
century and a Palestinian ascetic in his latter
years. It survives in Cyril's extant works. The
Menaion and several manuscripts ascribe this hymn to
Germanos; others attribute it to Byzantios and one
claims Theodore the Studite as author.

Euthemius the Great (Jan. 20)
at Vespers

Be of good cheer, said the angel of
the Lord to the parents,
because a child will be born to you
from your loins,
bearing the name of cheerfulness;
thus he brought to them the
proclamation of the birth;
5   and from infancy, Father Euthemius,
you were reared together with prayer.

MHN ΦΕΒΡΟΥΑΡΙΟΣ

Τῆ Β' ΤΗΣ ΥΠΑΠΑΝΤΗΣ (ἐις τὸν ἑσπερινόν)

I.

'Ως ὡράθης, Χριστέ,
ὡς λαβίδι χερσὶ
τῶς σὲ τεκούσης ἐπεδόθης
τῷ πρεσβύτῃ Συμεὼν βρέφος τέλειον
5   ἄνθραξ μὴ φλέγων γινωσκόμενος,
       ἀκατάληπτε
όθεν θείαις ἀγκάλαις κατέχων σε
ἠγαλλιᾶτο νεάζων τῷ πνεύματι
καὶ τὴν λύσιν ἐπεζήτει, σῶτερ, βοῶν
       σοι
νῦν ἀπολύεις με τὸν σὸν
10   δοῦλον, κατὰ τὸ ῥῆμά σου,
τῆς προσκαίρου πρὸς αἰώνιον
ζωήν· σαρκὶ γὰρ εἰδόν σε.

February 2 is known in the Eastern Church as the
feast of the Presentation of Christ in the Temple
(Ὑπαπαντῆ). It is commonly called the Meeting,
signifying the meeting of Christ with His chosen
people in the person of Simeon the Elder. It is
counted among the twelve major feasts of the Eastern
Church. This holiday concludes the Nativity sequence
that starts on November 15, the beginning of the
Christmas fast. In the Western Church this feast day
celebrates three events: the Purification of the
Virgin, the Presentation of Christ in the Temple, and
Candlemas.

Just as in the hymns for Christmas and the
Epiphany, the emphasis of the hymns is on Christ's
condescension for the sake of humanity; the lawgiver
becoming obedient to the Law. The text of the hymns,
for the most part, is based on the passage of Luke 2:
22-40 and all echo Simeon's song, Nunc Dimittis.
Kassia's hymns follow the established pattern of the
other hymns for that day. These three works exist in
only one Mt. Athos manuscript, Cod Θ 32, that was
found and transcribed by Eustratiades, "Κασιανή ἡ
Μελωδός," pp. 107-08.

FEBRUARY

The Meeting of the Lord (Feb. 2)
at Vespers

I.

When you appeared Christ,
in the arms of her who bore you
as in a pair of tongs
you were given to Simeon the Elder a
    perfect child,
5   a coal perceived not burning;
when he held you in his arms
he rejoiced full of youthful spirit
and asked for release, "Savior," he
    cried out to you,
"now release me, your servant,
10   from this world to eternal life,
according to your word,
for I have seen you in human form."

lines 2-3. The term "pair of tongs" is from
Isaiah 6:6-7. It is frequently used to describe the
Virgin's arms presenting Christ to the Elder Simeon.

line 5. This is a reference to Isaiah who
foresaw Christ as a coal of fire, Isaiah 6:1-12,
which is often used as a symbol for Christ.

line 9. Cf. Luke 2:29-30.

II.

　　　　　'Η Παρθένος ἁγνὴ
　　　　　τὸν ἐξ αὐτῆς σωματωθέντα
　　　　　περιφέρουσα χερσὶν ἐπιδίδωσι
　　　　　θείῳ πρεσβύτῃ δέξαι, λέγουσα, ὄν
　　　　　　ἐδήλωσε
5　　　　προφητῶν ἁγίων κηρύγματα
　　　　　βρέφος δι' οἶκτον νυνὶ χρεματίσαντα
　　　　　καὶ ὡς θεῖον νομοδότην πληροῦντα νόμον
　　　　　καὶ ἀναβόησον αὐτῷ·
　　　　　ἦλθες ὁ ἀπολύων με
10　　　τῆς προσκαίρου πρὸς αἰώνιον
　　　　　ζωήν, Κύριε, δόξα σοι.

III.

　　　　　Πῶς σε βρέφος κρατῶ
　　　　　τὸν συνοχέα τῶν ἁπάντων
　　　　　πῶς προσάγω σε ναῷ ὑπεράγαθε,
　　　　　πῶς ταῖς ἀγκάλαις τοῦ πρεσβύτου σε
5　　　　ἐπιδίδωμι τὸν πατρῴοις κόλποις
　　　　　　καθήμενον
　　　　　πῶς καθαρσίων ἠνέσχου ὁ ἅπασαν
　　　　　ρυπωθεῖσαν ἀποκαθαίρων φύσιν;
　　　　　ὁ θεοχώρητος ναὸς
　　　　　ἔφη ἡ ἀπειρόγαμος
10　　　τὴν πολλήν σου συγκατάβασιν,
　　　　　Χριστέ, ἀποθαυμάζουσα.

II.

The undefiled Virgin
carrying in her arms
him whom she embodied
delivers him to the holy elder,
      saying,
5 "Receive him whom the teachings
of the prophets proclaimed,
the child who because of compassion is
      now summoned
and as the holy lawgiver fulfills the
      law";
and he cried out to him;
10 "You have come who will release me
from this world to eternal life;
glory to you, Lord."

III.

"How can I hold you as a child,
you who holds everything together?
How do I bring you to the temple, who
      is beyond goodness?
How do I deliver you to the arms of
      the elder
5 who sits in the bosom of the Father?
How do you endure purification,
you who purifies the whole corrupt
      nature?"
So said the Virgin
the temple who contained God
10 marveling at your great condescension,
Christ.

42   Menaia

Τῇ Ε' ΑΓΑΘΗΣ ΜΑΡΤΨΡΟΣ (ἐις τόν ἐσπερινόν)

       Παράδοξον θαῦμα γέγονεν
       ἐν τῇ ἀθλήσει τῆς πανενδόξου Ἀγάθης
       καὶ Μάρτυρος Χριστοῦ τοῦ Θεοῦ
         ἐφάμιλλον τῷ Μωϋσεῖ·
       ἐχεῖνος γὰρ τὸν λαὸν νομοθετῶν ἐν τῷ
         ὄρει,
5   τὰς ἐγγραφείσας ἐν πλαξὶ
       θεοχαράχτους Γραφὰς ἐδέξατο·
       ἐνταῦθα δὲ ὁ Ἄγγελος οὐρανόθεν
       τῷ τάφῳ πλάκα ἐπεκόμισεν
       ἐγγεγραμμένην·
10   Νοῦς ὅσιος, αὐτοπροαίρετος,
       τιμὴ ἐκ Θεοῦ, καὶ πατρίδος λύτρωσις.

Agathe was a pious Christian, a noble maiden who lived during the reign of Decius (249-51). She was persecuted by Quintianus, the consul of Sicily, for refusing his amorous advances and remaining unshakable in her faith and her chastity. When she expired from the tortures and was placed in a tomb, an angel from heaven appeared and placed a tablet upon her tomb. On it was the inscription quoted in the hymn. The author regards this phenomenon equal to the one that occurred when Moses received the Decalogue on Mt. Sinai (Cf. Exodus, 18-24; 32-34). The Menaion and several manuscripts attribute the hymn to a certain Sykeotes.

Martyr Agathe (Feb. 5)
at Vespers

An incredible wonder occurred
at the martyrdom of the all-glorious
      Agathe
and martyr of Christ, God, one equal
      to Moses';
for he framed the laws of his people
      on the mountain,
5   when he received the God-written
      Commandments
inscribed on a tablet;
in this instance, an angel from heaven
placed a tablet on her tomb
on which was inscribed:
10   "Holy mind, possessed of free choice,
honor from God, and deliverance of the
      country."

ΜΗΝ ΜΑΡΤΙΟΣ

Τῇ Α΄ ΕΥΔΟΚΙΑΣ ΤΗΣ ΑΠΟ ΣΑΜΑΡΕΙΤΩΝ (εἰς τὸν ἑσπερινόν)

Καταλιποῦσα τὰ τερπνὰ καὶ ποικίλα τοῦ
βίου
ἡ Ὁσία καὶ Μάρτυς,
καὶ σταυρὸν ἀραμένη ἐπ' ὤμων,
προσῆλθε τοῦ νυμφευθῆναί σοι, Χριστὲ,
5   καὶ σὺν οἰμωγαῖς δακρύων ἐβόα·
Μή με τὴν πόρνην ἀπορρίψῃς,
ὁ ἀσώτους καθαίρων·
μή μου τὰ δάκρυα παρίδῃς τῶν δεινῶν
ὀρλημάτων·
ἀλλὰ δέξαι με ὥσπερ τὴν πόρνην ἐκείνην
10   τὴν τὸ μύρον σοι προσενέγκασαν,
καὶ ἀκούσω κἀγὼ
Ἡ πίστις σου σέσωκέ σε,
πορεύου εἰς εἰρήνην.

MARCH

Eudokia, also known as Eudokia of the Samarians, was a harlot like Mary Magdalene, and, like her, she repented and became a follower of Christ. She lived a very severe ascetic life, and was martyred around A.D. 126, during the reign of Hadrian (117-38). The hymn, beginning in line 5, echoes the words of Kassia's hymn on Mary Magdalene that is sung at vespers on Holy Wednesday. Three manuscripts attribute this hymn to Kassia. Most manuscripts and the Menaion claim it is the work of John the Monk.

Eudokia of the Samarians (March 1)
at Vespers

The pious and martyred one
left behind the pleasures and
    complexities of life,
and lifting the cross on her
    shoulders,
came to be wed to you, Christ,
5   and with wails of tears cried out,
"Don't cast me, the harlot, aside,
you who purges the dissolute;
don't overlook my tears for my debts,
but receive me as you did that harlot
10   who brought myrrh to you,
so I too might hear:
'Your faith has saved you,
go in peace'."

line 9. The reference is to Mary Magdalene, the
sinful penitent woman who washed Christ's feet with
her tears and wiped them dry with her hair. Luke 7:
36-50.

lines 12-13. Luke 7:50.

Τῇ ΚΕ' ΤΟΥ ΕΥΑΓΓΕΛΙΣΜΟΥ (εἰς τὸν
ἐσπερινόν)

Ἀπεστάλη ἄγγελος Γαβριήλ,
οὐρανόβεν ἐκ Θεοῦ,
πρὸς παρθένον ἀμόλυντον,
εἰς πόλιν τῆς Γαλιλαίας Ναζαρέτ,
5   εὐαγγελίσασθαι αὐτῇ τοῦ ξένου τρόπου
τὴν σύλληψιν.
Ἀπεστάλη δοῦλος ἀσώματος
πρὸς τὴν ἔμψυχον πόλιν καὶ πύλεν
νοεράν,
μηνῦσαι δεσποτικῆς παρουσίας τὴν
συγκατάβασιν·
Ἀπεστάλη στρατιώτης οὐράνιος,
10   πρὸς τὸ ἄχραντον τῆς δόξης παλάτιον,
προετοιμάσαι τῷ Κτίστῃ κατοικίαν
ἄληκτον
καὶ προσελθὼν πρὸς αὐτὴν ἐκραύγαζε.
Χαῖρε, θρόνε πυρίμορφε
τῶν τετραμόρφων ὑπερενδοξοτέρα·
15   Χαῖρε, καθέδρα βασιλικὴ οὐράνιε·
χαῖρε, ὄρος ἀλατόμητον,
δοχεῖον πανέντιμον.
ἐν σοὶ γὰρ πᾶν τὸ πλήρωμα κατῴκησε
τῆς θεότητος σωματικῶς,
20   εὐδοκίᾳ Πατρὸς ἀιδίου
καὶ συνεργείᾳ τοῦ Παναγίου Πνεύματος·
Χαῖρε, κεχαριτωμένη,
ὁ Κύριος μετὰ σοῦ.

line 14. The reference is to the four
creatures, each with four wings and four faces in the
vision of Ezekiel 1:5-6, and to the four creatures of
the Book of Revelation 4:6-9, influenced by Ezekiel.
Both references suggest the coming of God and his
intervention in human affairs.
    lines 15-17. The Annunciation of the Virgin
Mary is considered by the Eastern Church as one of
the twelve great religious feasts. On that day Mary
is honored for freely accepting the vocation for
which she had been foreordained by God. As the
Mother of the Lord, it was through her, serving as
the instrument of God, that the hypostatic union
between God and man occurred. To illustrate this
fact vividly, many titles are given to her in the

The Annunciation of the Most Holy Theotokos
(March 25) at Vespers

The angel Gabriel
was sent from heaven by God
to an undefiled virgin,
to a city of Galilee, Nazareth,
5   to announce to her the strange manner
of her conception.
The bodiless servant was sent
to the living city and the spiritual
gate
to make known the descent of the
Master's presence.
The heavenly soldier was sent
10   to the spotless palace of glory
to prepare the everlasting dwelling
for the creator.
And coming before her he proclaimed:
"Hail, fiery throne
more glorious by far than the fourfold
form living beings.
15   Hail, heavenly royal seat.
Hail unhewn mountain,
most honored vessel.
For in you has come to dwell bodily
the fullness of the Godhead,
20   by the good will of the everlasting
Father
and with the joint cooperation of the
Holy Spirit.
Hail you who are favored
The Lord is with you."

services of the feast day. Among them are those
found in this hymn, "heavenly royal seat" or throne,
"unhewn," i.e., pure or untouched, and "honored
vessel." Because of the importance of the feast day,
numerous hymns, some very lengthy, have been written
about the occasion. However, Kassia's hymn surpasses
the ordinary Byzantine Salutations to the Virgin with
its very effective short and to the point beginning,
and its terseness and simplicity. Thirteenth-century
manuscripts attribute the words and melody to Kassia.
A later fourteenth-century manuscript attributes it
to Anatolius, and the Menaion claims it is anonymous.

48 Menaia

MHN ΑΠΡΙΛΙΟΣ

Τῇ Α' ΜΑΡΙΑΣ ΤΗΣ ΑΙΓΥΠΤΙΑΣ (εἰς τὸν ἐσπερινόν)

Τὰ τῆς ψυχῆς θηρεύματα
καὶ τὰ πάθη τῆς σαρκὸς
τῷ ξίρει τῆς ἐγκρατείας ἔτεμες·
τὰ τῆς ἐννοίας ἐγκλήματα
5   τῇ σιγῇ τῆς ἀσκήσεως ἀπέπνιξας,
καὶ ῥείθροις τῶν δακρύων σου
τὴν ἔρημον ἅπασαν κατήρδευσας,
καὶ ἐβλάστησας ἡμῖν τῆς μετανοίας
    καρπούς
διό σου τὴν μνήμην, Ὁσία, ἑορτάζομεν.

APRIL

Mary the Egyptian went to Alexandria at the age
of twelve and for the next seventeen years lived a
life of sin. One day when the people of the city
were setting out for Jerusalem to celebrate the feast
of the Exaltation of the Holy Cross, she decided to
accompany them. When the group arrived in Jerusalem
all except her entered the church without hindrance.
She was held back by a great invisible force.
Realizing that this was the result of her sinful
life, she cried bitter tears and prayed to God to
permit her to enter. In return she promised to
renounce the world and to live a chaste life. This
prayer renewed her courage to enter the church, which
she did without hindrance. After venerating the
cross she left that same day for the farthest ends of
the desert. She lived there for forty-seven years in
a hermetic, ascetic life that was beyond human
endurance and in continuous prayer. Near the end of
her life, she met a certain abbot named Zosimas who
happened to be traveling through the desert. She
confessed her whole life to him and asked that he
administer to her the sacrament of Communion.
Zosimas complied and promised to return the next year
on Holy Thursday with the holy Eucharist. When the
abbot returned the following year, he found her dead
stretched out on the sand, and beside her was an
inscription written in the sand: "Abba Zosima, bury
the body of the wretched Mary. I died the day I

Mary the Egyptian (April 1)
at Vespers

You severed the temptations of the
    soul
and the passions of the body
with the sword of temperance;
the crimes of the mind
you choked with the silence of
    spiritual discipline,
and with streams of your tears
you watered the entire desert,
and made to grow in us the seeds of
    repentance:
therefore we celebrate your memory,
    holy one.

5

---

received the Holy Communion. Pray for me." She died
in 378. Some hagiographical sources list her date of
death as 437. The Menaion claims the hymn as
anonymous, and three manuscripts attribute it to a
Studite monk.

ΜΗΝ ΙΟΥΝΙΟΣ

Τῇ ΚΔ΄ ΓΕΝΕΘΛΙΟΝ ΙΩΑΝΝΟΥ ΤΟΥ ΒΑΠΤΙΣΤΟΥ (εἰς τὸν
                        ἑσπερινόν)

Ἡσαΐου νῦν τοῦ Προφήτου ἡ φωνὴ
σήμερον ἐν τῇ τοῦ μείζονος Προφητῶν
        κυήσει,
Ἰωάννου, πεπλήρωται·
Ἰδοὺ γὰρ, φησὶν, ἀποστελῶ τὸν
        Ἄγγελόν μου πρὸ προσώπου σου,
5   ὃς κατασκευάσει τὴν ὁδόν σου ἔμπροσθέν
        σου.
Οὗτος οὖν ὁ τοῦ ἐπουρανίου Βασιλέως
        στρατιώτης προδραμὼν,
ὡς ἀληθῶς εὐθείας ἐποίει τὰς τρίβους
        τοῦ Θεοῦ ἡμῶν,
ἄνθρωπος μὲν τῇ φύσει, Ἄγγελος δὲ τὸν
        βίον ὑπάρχων·
ἀγνείαν γὰρ παντελῆ καὶ σωφροσύνην
        ἀσπασάμενος
10   εἶχε μὲν τὸ κατὰ φύσιν, ἔφυγε δὲ τὸ
        παρὰ φύσιν
ὑπὲρ φύσιν ἀγωνισάμενος.
Αὐτὸν, ἅπαντες πιστοὶ, ἐν ἀρεταῖς
        μιμούμενοι,
πρεσβεύειν ὑπὲρ ἡμῶν δυσωπήσωμεν
εἰς τὸ σωθῆναι τὰς ψυχὰς ἡμῶν.

JUNE

A hymn commemorating the birth of St. John the
Baptist and forerunner of Christ.   It discusses St.
John's virtuous life and his fulfillment of the Old
Testament prophecy.

Birth of St. John the Baptist (June 24)
at Vespers

Now the voice of Isaiah the prophet
this day has been fulfilled
by the conception of one greater than
the prophet, John.
For behold, he said, I will send my
messenger before your
countenance,
5   who shall prepare your way.
He then, as soldier and forerunner of
the Heavenly King,
truly made straight the paths of our
God,
being a man by nature, but an angel in
his life.
For he had embraced complete chastity
and self-restraint,
10   he held to that which was according to
nature, but avoided that which
was contrary to nature,
striving beyond nature.
Let us all, the faithful, imitate him
in virtue,
implore him to plead on our behalf
for the saving of our souls.

lines 4-5. Malachias 3:1; Matthew 11:9-11.
lines 6-7. Isaiah 40:3.

Τῇ ΚΘ' ΠΕΤΡΟΥ ΚΑΙ ΠΑΥΛΟΥ (ἐις τὸν ἑσπερινόν)

Τοὺς φωστῆρας τοὺς μεγάλους τῆς
      Ἐκκλησίας,
Πέτρον καὶ Παῦλον, εὐφημήσωμεν·
Ὑπὲρ ἥλιον γὰρ ἔλαμψαν
ἐν τῷ τῆς πίστεως στερεώματι,
5   καὶ τὰ ἔθνη ταῖς ἀκτῖσι τοῦ κηρύγματος
ἐκ τῆς 'αγνοίας ἐπανήγαγον.
Ὁ μὲν τῷ σταυρῷ προσηλωθεὶς
πρὸς οὐρανὸν τὴν πορείαν ἐποιήσατο,
ἔνθα τῆς βασιλείας
10   παρὰ Χριστοῦ τὰς κλεῖς ἐγκεχείρισται.
Ὁ δὲ τῷ ξίφει ἀποτμηθεὶς
πρὸς τὸν Σωτῆρα ἐκδημήσας
ἐπαξίως μακαρίζεται.
καὶ ἀμφότεροι τὸν Ἰσραὴλ
      καταγγέλλουσιν
15   ὡς εἰς αὐτὸν τὸν Κύριον
χεῖρας ἀδίκως ἐκτείναντα.
Διὸ εὐχαῖς αὐτῶν,
Χριστὲ ὁ Θεὸς ἡμῶν, τοὺς καθ' ἡμῶν
      κατάβαλε
καὶ τὴν ὀρθόδοξον πίστιν κράτυνον
ὡς φιλάνθρωπος.

Saints Peter and Paul are considered by the
Eastern Church as missionary luminaries of early
Christianity. Individually, both spent their lives
traveling throughout the Graeco-Roman world, Asia
Minor and Asia, preaching the Gospel. Both were
martyred for their Christian devotion in Rome during
the reign of Nero (circa A.D. 64-66). Peter was
crucified and hung head down; Paul was beheaded
shortly after Peter had been crucified.

SS. Peter and Paul (June 29)
        at Vespers

Let us praise Peter and Paul
the great luminaries of the Church;
for they outshone the sun
in the firmness of their faith,
5   and brought back the nations from the
darkness of ignorance by the rays of
        the Gospel.
The one, nailed to the cross,
made his way to heaven,
where he received from Christ
10   the keys of the Kingdom.
The other, cut off by the sword,
went forth to the savior,
and is worthily blessed.
And both accuse Israel
15   as having stretched out its hands
unjustly against the Lord.
Therefore by their prayers,
Christ our God, cast down those who
        are against us
and strengthen the true faith
in your love for mankind.

MHN IOYΛIOΣ

Τῇ Κ' ΗΛΙΟΥ ΤΟΥ ΠΡΟΦΗΤΟΥ (ἐις τὸν ὄρθρον)

Τῶν Προφητῶν τοὺς ἀκραίμονας
καὶ παμφαεῖς φωστῆρας τῆς οἰκουμένης
ἐν ὕμνοις τιμήσωμεν, πιστοί,
'Ηλίαν καὶ 'Ελισσαῖον·
5   καὶ Χριστῷ ἐκβοήσωμεν χαρμονικῶς·
Εὔσπλαγχνε Κύριε, παράσχου τῷ λαῷ σου
ἰκεσίαις τῶν Προφητῶν σου
ἄφεσιν ἁμαρτιῶν
καὶ τὸ μέγα ἔλεος.

JULY

Elijah is often considered the founder of the
prophetic movement in Israel and one of its most
prominent prophets. His power and greatness are
indicated by the numerous legends that have been
written about him, beginning with the ancient Hebrew
historians. Moreover, according to Biblical
tradition, only two men, Enoch (Genesis 5:24) and
Elijah, were worthy of ascending to God without
having to die (Kings 2:11-12). Further proof of his
power and importance is the fact that he alone with
Moses appeared talking with Christ as his
Transfiguration (Matthew 17:1-8; Mark 9:2-8; Luke 9:
28-36). The Eastern Church considers the Prophet
Elijah among the ranks of the saints and honors him
along with his pupil and successor Elisha on July 20,
the day, according to legend, that he was taken up by
God. Some manuscripts attribute the hymn to
Byzantios; the Menaion claims it is anonymous.

The Prophet Elijah (July 20)
             at the Orthos

           Faithful, let us honor with hymns
           Elijah and Elisha,
           the topmost branches of the Prophets
           and radiant luminaries of the
                universe;
5   and let us joyfully call out to
                Christ:
           Merciful Lord, grant to your people
           the remission of sins
           and great mercy
           through the prayers of your Prophets.

     line 3. The most eminent of the prophets
because of the various miracles which they both
worked, Cf. 1 Kings 16:29-22; 2 Kings 1-2:25.

Τῇ ΚΔ' ΧΡΙΣΤΙΝΗΣ ΜΑΓΑΛΟΜΑΡΤΥΡΟΣ (εἰς τὸν ὄρθρον)

I.

          Δοξάζομέν σου, Χριστέ, τὴν πολλὴν
            εὐσπλαγχνίαν
          καὶ τὴν ἀγαθότητα τὴν εἰς ἡμᾶς
            γενομένην,
          ὅτι καὶ γυναῖκες κατήργησαν τὴν πλάνην
            τῆς εἰδωλομανίας
          δυνάμει τοῦ σταυροῦ σου, φιλάνθρωπε·
5   τύραννον οὐκ ἐπτοήθησαν, τὸν δόλιον
            κατεπάτησαν,
          ἴσχυσαν δὲ ὀπίσω σου ἐλθεῖν
          εἰς ὀσμὴν μύρου σου ἔδραμον
          πρεσρεύουσαι ὑπὲρ τῶν ψυχῶν ἡμῶν.

_____

    These five hymns are sung towards the end of the
Orthos, after the Lauds or morning psalms.
Christina, a native of Tyre in Phoenicia, was the
beautiful daughter of Urbanus, a general in the army
of the Emperor Severus (A.D. 193-211). At a very
young age and without the knowledge of her parents,
she became a Christian, and it was claimed that she
helped to convert to Christianity close to 3,000
people. When news of her Christian activities
reached her father, he imposed on her the harshest
and cruelest tortures. She was finally speared to
death and decapitated by the public executioner in
A.D. 200. The hymns celebrate her unwavering faith
in Christ in the face of all the sufferings. The
Menaion claims Byzantios the author of the first hymn
and the others as anonymous. One manuscript
attributes the first hymn to John the Monk; most
manuscripts attribute the second either to Byzantios
or Anatolios; the fourth to Cyprianos; and the fifth
to either George of Nicodemia or Cyprianos.

The Great-martyr Christina (July 24)
at the Orthos

I.

We praise your great mercy, Oh Christ,
and your goodness to us,
because even women have abandoned the
error of idol-mania
by the power of your cross, friend of
mankind;

5   they were not frightened by the
oppressor, but trampled the
deceiver,
they were strong to follow behind you
and they quickly moved to the scent of
your myrrh
interceding on behalf of our souls.

lines 6-7. An allusion to the three myrrh-
bearing women, the faithful followers of Christ who
went to his tomb to anoint his body. Following their
example, other women, among them Christina, joined
the ranks of the faithful. The hymn praises the
courage and staunch faith of all the women who had
become followers of Christ.

II.

'Όλρον λιποῦσα πατρικόν, Χριστὸν
    ποθοῦσα εἰλικρινῶς,
δόξαν εὕρατο ἡ μάρτυς καὶ πλοῦτον
    οὐράνιον,
καὶ τῇ παντευχίᾳ περιπεφραγμένη τῆς
    πίστεως
τῷ ὅπλῳ τοῦ σταυροῦ κατεπάτησε τὸν
    τύραννον
5   ὅθεν ἄγγελοι τοὺς ἀγῶνας θαυμαζοντες
    ἔλεγον
"Πέπτωκεν ὁ ἐχθρὸς ὑπο γυναικὸς
    ἡττηθείς
στεφανῖτις ἀνεδείχθη ἡ μάρτυς
καὶ Χριστὸς εἰς αἰῶνας βασιλεύει ὡς
    θεός,
ὁ παρέχων τῷ κόσμῳ τὸ μέγα ἔλεος".

III.

'Εθαυματούργησε, Χριστέ,
τοῦ σταυροῦ σου ἡ δύναμις,
ὅτι καὶ Χριστίνα ἡ μάρτυς
ἀθλητικὸν ἀγῶνα ἠγωνίσατο
5   ὅθεν τὸ ἀσθενὲς τῆς φύσεως
    ἀπυρριψαμένη
γενναίως ἀντέστης κατὰ τῶν τυράννων·
διὸ καὶ τὸ βραρεῖον τῆς νίκης
    κομισαμένη
πρεσβεύεις ὑπὲρ τῶν ψυχῶν ἡμῶν.

II.

Leaving the wealth of her family, and
      longing sincerely for Christ,
the martyr found heavenly glory and
      riches,
and totally shielded with the armour
      of faith,
and the weapon of the Cross, trampled
      the oppressor;
5   therefore angels amazed at her
      struggles, said:
"The enemy has fallen, defeated by a
      woman;
the martyr, crowned, was lifted upward
and Christ reigns as God to all
      eternity,
who gives to the world his great
      mercy."

III.

Christ, the power of your cross
has worked wondrous deeds,
because Christina the martyr
also contended in mighty contest;
5   whereby, throwing off the weakness of
      her nature
she bravely withstood the oppressors;
therefore, carrying off the prize of
      victory,
she intercedes on behalf of our souls.

IV.

                  Σταυρὸν ὡς ὅπλον κραταιόν,
                  Χριστίνα μάρτυς, κατέχουσα χερσὶ
                  τὴν πίστιν ὡς θώρακα, ἐλπίδα θυρεόν,
                  ἀγάπην τόξον, τῶν τυράννων
  5   τὰς τιμωρίας ἐνίκησας ἀνδρείως,
                  τῶν δαιμόνων τὰς πανουργίας κατήργησας
                      ἐνθέως
                  τὴν κεφαλὴν δὲ τμηθεῖσα χορεύεις ἐν
                      Χριστῷ
                  ἀδιαλείπτως πρεσβεύουσα ὑπὲρ τῶν ψυχῶν
                      ἡμῶν.

V.

                  Τῇ παρθενικῇ σου θελχθεὶς ὡραιότητι
                  ὁ Βασιλεὺς τῆς δόξης, Χριστός,
                  ὡς ἀμώμητόν σε νύμφην ἑαυτῷ ἡρμόσατο
                      συναρείᾳ ἀκηράτῳ.
                  Ἐν γὰρ τῷ θελήματι αὐτοῦ
  5   παρασχόμενος τῷ κάλλει σου δύναμιν,
                  κατ' ἐχθρῶν τε καὶ παθῶν ἀήττητον
                      ἔδειξεν
                  ἐγκαρτερήσασαν δὲ αἰκίαις πικραῖς καὶ
                      βασάνοις δριμυτάταις,
                  διπλῷ στέφει δισσῶς σε κατέστεψε,
                  καὶ παρέστησεν ἐκ δεξιῶν αὐτοῦ
 10   ὡς βασίλισσαν πεποικιλμένην.
                  Αὐτὸν δυσώπησον, Παρθένομάρτυς
                      Χριστώνυμε,
                  τοῖς ὑμνηταῖς σου δοθῆναι
                  σωτηρίαν καὶ ζωὴν καὶ μέγα ἔλεος.

IV.

> Christina the martyr, holding the
> > cross
> in her hand as a mighty weapon,
> with faith as a breast plate, hope as
> > a shield,
> love as bow, bravely overcame
5 > the punishments of her oppressors,
> divinely defeated the evilness of the
> > demons;
> although beheaded, you are glorified
> > in Christ,
> unceasingly interceding on behalf of
> > our souls.

V.

> Christ, the King of Glory,
> fascinated by your maidenly beauty,
> joined you to him as an unblemished
> > bride in a pure union.
> And because he willed it,
5 > he provided strength along with your
> > beauty,
> that proved unconquerable against both
> > enemies and passions.
> It remained firm under bitter assaults
> > and the most savage tortures.
> he doubly crowned you, with a twofold
> > wreath,
> and placed you at his right
10 > as a much adorned queen.
> Entreat him, Virgin-Martyr Bearing
> > Christ's name,
> to grant to those who sing your praise
> salvation, life and great mercy.

line 8. i.e. Christina was endowed with both
beauty and great strength of will. She remained true
to her faith till the end. She was crowned a martyr
and given a place by the right hand of Christ.

line 11. Χριστώνυμε - Bearing Christ's name,
i.e., the root of Christina's name is Christ.

ΜΗΝ ΑΥΓΟΥΣΤΟΣ

Τῇ Α' ΤΩΝ ΑΓΙΩΝ ΜΑΚΚΑΒΑΙΩΝ (εἰς τὸν ἑσπερινόν)

Ψυχαὶ δικαίων ἐν χειρὶ Κυρίου,
καθάπερ Ἀβραὰμ καὶ Ἰσαὰκ καὶ Ἰακὼβ,
οἱ πρὸ νόμου προπάτορες καὶ Μακκαβαίων
    πρόγονοι,
τῶν νῦν εὐφημουμένων παρ' ἡμῶν.
5   Οὗτοι γὰρ οἱ καρτερόψυχοι Ἀβραμιαῖοι
        ὑπάρχοντες
    τὴν πίστιν ἐζήλωσαν τοῦ ἑαυτῶν
        προπάτορος Ἀβραάμ,
    καὶ μέχρι θανάτου ἠγωνίσαντο δι'
        εὐσέβειαν·
    εὐσεβῶς γὰρ συντραφέντες,
    καὶ ἐννόμως συναθλήσαντες,
10 τὴν ἀσέβειαν διήλεγξαν τοῦ ἐπαράτου
        Ἀντιόχου
    καὶ μηδὲν προτιμήσαντες τῶν τῆς
        παρούσης ζωῆς
    διὰ τὴν αἰώνιον,

AUGUST

    This hymn praises the martyrdom of the ninety-
year-old priest/philosopher Eleazar and the seven
brothers and their mother who preferred to die rather
than disobey the Jewish Law. They are called
Maccabees because their martyrdom occurred during the
early days of the Maccabean revolt (ca. 168 B.C.) and
because their sufferings and triumphs are related in
the Old Testament apocryphal and pseudepigraphal
books of Maccabees. A short version is found in the
apocryphal second book of Maccabees (6:18-7: 42) and
a detailed account is in the pseudepigraphal book of
four Maccabees (5:4-17: 6), on which this hymn is
based. These martyrs have nothing to do with the
Maccabean heroes of the revolt (ca. 168-142 B.C.).
The hymn gives the name of the mother as Solomone.

AUGUST
The Holy Maccabees (Aug. 1)
at Vespers

The souls of the righteous are in the
    hand of the Lord,
just like Abraham and Isaac and Jacob,
the forefathers before the Law and
    ancestors of the Maccabees,
who are now being praised by us.
5   For these strong-spirited beings,
        descendants of Abraham
imitated the faith of their forefather
    Abraham,
and struggled until death for
    religious devotion;
for they were reared devoutly,
and lawfully struggled together;
10 they refuted the impiety of the
        accursed Antiochus;
and never preferred the things of the
    present life
over the eternal one;

line 10.   Antiochus IV Epiphanes (177-164 B.C.),
who proscribed Judaism and persecuted the Jews who
refused to follow his orders.

This is a later Christian addition; she is nameless
in 2 Maccabees and 4 Maccabees. In the Greek account
she is called Solomone, while in the Syrian she is
Shamone and/or Maryam.
    The book of 4 Maccabees, and especially the
account of the martyrs, had a profound and widespread
influence among the early Church Fathers, East and
West.   In particular, the Eastern Fathers looked upon
the Jewish martyrs as Christian proto-martyrs, and
many panegyrics were written on them.   Gregory
Nazianzus (329-90 A.D.) in his oration on the martyrs
considers them worthy of universal honor and assigns
the first day of August as the annual day of their
commemoration.   The Eastern Church continues to honor
their memory on that day.
    The Menaion and two manuscripts attribute the
hymn to Cosmos the Monk.

πάντα Θεῷ ἀνέθεντο,
ψυχὴν, ἀνδρείαν, αἴσθησιν, σῶμα ἁπαλὸν
15   καὶ ἀμοιβὰς τῶν ἁγνείᾳ τεθραμμένων.
Ὦ ῥίζης εὐσεβοῦς!
ἐξ ἧς ὑμεῖς ἐβλαστήσατε, Μακκαβαῖοι.
Ὦ μητρὸς ἁγίας!
τῆς τεξαμένης τὸν ἰσάριθμον τῆς
      ἑβδομάδος ἀριθμόν.
20   Ἀλλ' ἱκετεύομεν ὑμᾶς, Μακκαβαῖοι,
σὺν τῇ μητρὶ ὑμῶν Σολομονῇ
καὶ τῷ σοφῷ ἱερεῖ Ἐλεαζάρῳ,
ὅταν παραστῆτε Χριστῷ τῷ Θεῷ,
δι' ὃν κεκοπιάκατε,
25   τοὺς πόνους τῶν καρπῶν ὑμῶν ἀπολαβεῖν
      παρ' αὐτοῦ,
ἐκτενῆ ἱκεσίαν ποιήσατε ὑπὲρ τῆς
      ἀνθρωπότητος·
ποιεῖ γὰρ ὅσα βούλεται,
καὶ πληροῖ τὰ θελήματα ὑμῶν
τῶν φοβουμένων αὐτον.

they devoted everything to God,
soul, bravery, feeling, tender body
15   and the benefit of having been raised
with a strict observance of
religious duties.
Oh pious root!
from which you were born, Maccabees.
Oh holy mother!
who brought forth children equal in
number to the days of the week.
20   But we beseech you, Maccabees,
with your mother Solomone
and the wise priest Eleazar,
when you stand before Christ the God,
for whom you have toiled,
25   to receive from him the fruits of your
labor,
perform a prolonged supplication on
behalf of mankind;
for he accomplishes whatever he wills,
and fulfills your wishes
who stand in awe of him.

line 19. Solomone bore seven sons. Their
brotherly love and sevenfold companionship during
their sufferings was compared to the seven days of
Creation (4 Macc. 14:7f.).

Τῇ ΙΕ΄ Η ΚΟΙΜΗΣΙΣ ΤΗΣ ΘΕΟΤΟΚΟΥ (εἰς τὸν ἑσπερινόν)

      Ὅτε ἐξεδήμησας, Θεοτόκε Παρθένε,
      πρὸς τὸν ἐκ σοῦ τεχθέντα ἀφράστως,
      παρῆν Ἰάκωβος ὁ Ἀδελφόθεος, καὶ
         πρῶτος Ἱεράρχης,
      Πέτρος τε, ἡ τιμιωτάτη κορυφαία τῶν
         Θεολόγων ἀκρότης,
5   καὶ σύμπας ὁ θεῖος τῶν Ἀποστόλων
         χορός,
      ἐκφαντορικαῖς θεολογίαις
      ὑμνολογοῦντες τὸ θεῖον καὶ ἐξαίσιον
      τῆς Χριστοῦ τοῦ Θεοῦ οἰκονομίας
         μυστήριον·
      καὶ τὸ ζωαρχικὸν καὶ θεοδόχον σου σῶμα
         κηδεύσαντες,
10   ἔχαιρον πανύμνητε.
      Ὑπερθεν δὲ
      αἱ πανάγιαι καὶ πρεοβύταται τῶν
         Ἀγγέλων Δυνάμεις
      τὸ θαῦμα ἐκπληττόμεναι,
      κεκυφυῖαι ἀλλήλαις ἔλεγον·

The "Dormition" or "Falling Asleep" of the
Theotokos (Mother of God) is known in the Western
Church as the Assumption. The texts for this holiday
are based primarily on non-scriptural sources.
According to tradition, the Theotokos was living in
the home of St. John on Mt. Zion at the time of her
death. The twelve Apostles were in different parts
of the world preaching. However, all, except Thomas,
were carried miraculously on a cloud to her bedside
so that they might see the Theotokos once again before her death. In addition to the Apostles, Paul
and the bishops Dionysios the Areopagite, Hierotheos
and Timothy were also present. As they stood around
her, the Theotokos gave up her spirit into the keep-
ing of her Son, and He Himself descended from heaven
and took her soul up with Him in His arms. In the
icons of the Dormition, Christ is seen standing above
the bier with Mary's soul resting in his arms, depic-
ted as a small child wrapped in white. After she gave
up her soul, the Apostles, led by Peter, sang funeral
hymns in her honor and carried her body to the valley
of Cedron near Gethsemane. There they placed her

The Dormition of the Theotokos (Aug. 15)
at Vespers

When you departed, O Virgin Theotokos,
to him who ineffably was born from
you,
James, the brother of the Lord and
first bishop was there,
and Peter, the honored leader and
chief of the theologians,
5   and the whole sacred fellowship of the
Apostles
in discourses revealing heavenly
things
sang the praises of the divine and
amazing mystery
of the dispensation of Christ our God;
and they rejoiced, O far-famed one,
10   as they buried your body, the life
originator and holder of God.
From heaven above,
the all-holy and most venerable of the
angelic powers
were amazed at the marvel,
bowed and said to one another:

line 4.   Peter was considered the first among
the Apostles.

---

body in a tomb especially prepared for her.   On the
third day after the burial, Thomas arrived anxious to
see the Theotokos for the last time.   The Apostles
opened the tomb and found it empty.   Like her Son,
she had risen from the dead and ascended into heaven.
This hymn is sung at the end of the Great Vespers
commemorating the Theotokos' dormition.
The hymn is attributed to several authors.
Three claim Kassia, two Byzantios, one the Patriarch
Germanos, another Cosmas, and the Menaion claims it
as anonymous.

15   Ἄρατε ὑμῶν τὰς πύλας,
        καὶ ὑποδέξασθε τὴν τεκοῦσαν τὸν
              οὐρανοῦ καὶ γῆς Ποιητήν·
        δοξολογίαις τε ἀνυμνήσωμεν
        τὸ σεπτὸν καὶ ἅγιον σῶμα,
        τὸ χωρῆσαν τὸν ἡμῖν
20   ἀθεώρητον καὶ Κύριον.
        Διό περ καὶ ἡμεῖς τὴν μνήμην σου
              ἑορτάζοντες,
        ἐκβοῶμεν σοι, Πανύμνητε
        Χριστιανῶν τὸ κέρας ὕψωσον,
        καὶ σῶσον τὰς ψυχὰς ἡμῶν.

15   "Open wide your gates,
            and receive her who bore the Creator
                    of heaven and earth;
            and with songs of praise let us
                    glorify
            her revered and holy body,
            the dwelling-place of the Lord
20   who is not to be seen by us."
            Therefore we too, as we celebrate your
                    feast day,
            cry out to you, O far-famed lady:
            "Raise up the Christian horn,
            and save our souls."

Τῇ ΚΣΤ′ ΑΔΡΙΑΝΟΥ ΚΑΙ ΝΑΤΑΛΙΑΣ   (εἰς τὸν ἑσπερινόν)

```
        Ὦ ζεῦγος ἄμωμον
        καὶ ἐκλεκτὸν τῷ Κυρίῳ
        ὦ συζυγία ἀρίστη
        καὶ μακαρία Θεῷ!
5       ὦ πεποθημένη δυὰς
        καὶ πεφιλημένη Χριστῷ!
        Τίς οὐκ ἐκπλαγῇ ἐν ταύτῳ
        ἀκουτισθεὶς
        τὰς τούτων ὑπὲρ ἄνθρωπον πράξεις!
10      πῶς τὸ θῆλυ ἠνδρίσατο
        κατὰ τοῦ πικροῦ τυράννου,
        καὶ τὸν ταύτης σύνευνον ἐνεύρωσε
        μὴ ὑπενδοῦναι τοῖς δεινοῖς,
        ἀλλ′ ὑπὲρ τῆς πίστεως ἑλέσθαι τὸ
              θανεῖν ὑπὲρ τὸ ζῆν;
15      Ὦ θεοπλόκων ῥημάτων
        Ναταλίας τῆς σοφῆς!
        ὦ παραινέσεων θείων τοὺς οὐρανοὺς
              διασχουσῶν,
        καὶ πρὸς αὐτὸν τὸν θρίνον τοῦ μεγάλου
              Βασιλέως
        Ἀδριανὸν τὸν ἔνδοξον γνώριμον
              καταστησασῶν!
20      Ἀλλ′ ὦ ξυνωρὶς ἁγία,
        ὑπὲρ ἡμῶν τῷ Θεῷ ἱκετεύσατε,
        τῶν ἐκ πόθου τελούντων τὴν μνήμην
              ὑμῶν,
        πειρασμῶν ῥυσθῆναι καὶ πάσης θλίψεως.
```

Adrianus and Natalia were a Christian couple
from Nicomedia. Initially, Adrianus was a military
officer at the imperial court of the emperor
Maximinus (308-14 A.D.), but was so moved by the
resolve of the Christians whom he saw being crucified
by the emperor that he became a Christian. For this
he was imprisoned and tortured. His wife, Natalia,
who had always been a Christian, secretly ministered
to him in prison and exhorted him not to weaken and
yield to the tortures. When his time to be martyred
arrived, she assisted at his cruel martyrdom with
heroic pride, to assure his glorious death. She died
shortly after her husband, but not a martyr's death.

Adrianus and Natalia (Aug. 26)
at Vespers

Oh perfect couple
and chosen by the Lord
oh excellent union
and blessed to God
5   oh regrettable pair
and beloved by Christ!
who was not amazed with this
when they heard
of their superhuman feats
10   how the woman played the man
against the bitter tyrant,
and she encouraged her husband
not to yield to the tortures
but to choose to die for the faith
rather than to live?
15   Oh God-inspired words
of the wise Natalia
oh divine exhortation that tore apart
the heavens,
and brought the esteemed disciple
Adrianus
to the very throne of the great King!
20   But oh holy couple,
intercede with God on our behalf,
to protect from temptation and all
afflictions
those who from love celebrate your
memory.

line 10. ἠνδρίσατο, "play the man," a term used
of a woman showing bravery.

line 19. i.e., the throne of Christ.

The Menaion lists the hymn as anonymous. In some
manuscripts it is attributed to Ephraim of Karia, and
others claim Kassia or Ephraim.

TRIODION

Τοῦ Τελώνου καὶ τοῦ Φαρισαίου

1.

Παντοκράτορ Κύριε, οἶδα, πόσα δύνανται
τὰ δάκρυα.
Ἐζεκίαν γὰρ ἐκ τῶν πυλῶν τοῦ θανάτου
ἀνήγαγον·
τὴν ἁμαρτωλὸν ἐκ τῶν χρονίων πταισμάτων
ἐρρύσαντο·
τὸν δὲ Τελώνην, ὑπὲρ τὸν Φαρισαῖον
ἐδικαίωσαν·
καὶ δέομαι, σὺν αὐτοῖς ἀριθμήσας·
Ἐλέησόν με.

2.

Ταῖς ἐξ ἔργων καυχήσεσι, Φαρισαῖον
δικαιοῦντα ἑαυτὸν κατέκρινας Κύριε,
καὶ Τελώνην μετριοπαθήσαντα,
καὶ στεναγμοῖς ἱλασμὸν αἰτούμενον,
ἐδικαίωσας·

5   οὐ γὰρ προσίεσαι, τοὺς μεγαλόφρονας
λογισμούς,
καὶ τὰς συντετριμμένας καρδίας, οὐκ
ἐξουθενεῖς·
διὸ καὶ ἡμεῖς σοὶ προσπίπτομεν, ἐν
ταπεινώσει,
τῷ παθόντι δι' ἡμᾶς
Παράσχου τὴν ἄφεσιν καὶ τὸ μέγα ἔλεος.

The Triodion constitutes the ten works of preparation, repentance and fasting preceding the festival of Easter in the Eastern Orthodox Church. It begins on the Sunday of the Publican and the Pharisee and ends the evening of Holy Saturday. The theme of the first two Sundays of this period is repentance or "metanoia," and it begins with the example of the Publican and the Pharisee (Lk. 7:36-50). The word "metanoia" in Greek means "change of mind," i.e., to change one's internal viewpoint and to attain a new way of looking at one's relationship to God and to others. The Pharisee had no desire to change his outlook; he was satisfied and complacent and thus allowed no chance of interaction between himself and God. The Publican, on the other hand, longed for a "change of mind," he was dissatisfied and longed for an inward

Sunday of the Publican and the Pharisee

1.

> Almighty Lord, I know how great is the
> power of tears.
> For they brought back Hezekiah from the
> gates of death;
> They delivered the sinful woman from
> many years of transgressions;
> They justified the Publican above the
> Pharisee.
> And I implore, number me among them;
> have mercy on me.

line 2. 4 Kings 20:1-6.
lines 3-4. Luke 7:36-50.

2.

> Lord, You have condemned the Pharisee
> who
> justified himself by boasting of his
> works,
> and You have justified the Publican who
> humbled himself
> and with cries of sorrow begged for
> mercy.
> 5   For you do not approve of proud-minded
> thoughts,
> and you do not disregard penitent
> hearts.
> Therefore, we too fall before You in
> humility,
> who has suffered for our sake.
> Grant us forgiveness and great mercy.

---

transformation. Christians are urged at the start of the Triodion to learn the secret of the Publican's inward self-dissatisfaction and thus prepare themselves for the Lenten journey.

The first hymn is sung at the beginning of the Vesper service on Saturday evening, and the second at the end of the Orthos on that Sunday. No author is given in the Triodion for either hymn. One manuscript claims the first hymn anonymous, another proclaims Stephanos Sabbaites as author, and still another, Anatolios. The second hymn is attributed to Stephanos Sabbaites in most manuscripts.

Τῇ Παρασκευῇ τῆς Α'. Εβδομάδος

    'Οργάνῳ χρησάμενος ὁ δυσμενής,
    τῷ συναποστάτῃ Τυράννῳ, δι' ἐπινοίας
      χαλεπῆς,
    τὸν νηστείᾳ καθαγνιζόμενον λαὸν εὐσεβῆ,
    τοῖς ἐκ μιαρῶν θυσιῶν κεχρημένοις
      βρώμασιν,
5   ἐπειρᾶτο καταμιαίνειν·
    ἀλλ αὐτὸς τὸ ἐκείνου μηχάνημα, σοφωτέρᾳ,
      διέλυσας ἐπινοίᾳ.
    ὄναρ ἐπιστάς, τῷ τότε 'Αρχιερεῖ,
    καὶ τὸ βαθὺ τῆς γνώμης ἀνακαλύπτων,
    καὶ τὸ ἄτοπον τοῦ ἐγχειρήματος ὑποδηλῶν·
10 καὶ δή σοι χαριστήρια θύοντες,
    σωτῆρα ἐπιγραφόμεθα,
    ἐτήσιον ἀνάμνησιν τοῦ γενομένου
      ποιούμενοι,
    καὶ τὸ λοιπὸν ἐξαιτούμενοι, τῶν ἐπινοιῶν
      τοῦ πονηροῦ,
    ἀβλαβεῖς περισώζεσθαι,
15 ταῖς πρὸς Θεόν σου πρεσβείαις,
    μεγαλομάρτυς Θεόδωρε.

According to tradition, the Emperor Julian the Apostate (361-63), as part of his campaign against the Christians, attempted to thwart their observance of the first week in Lent by ordering all the food for sale in the markets of Constantinople to be sprinkled with blood from pagan sacrifices. However, St. Theodore appeared in a dream to the Archbishop of the city, Eudoxius, warned him of the plot, and ordered him to warn all the Christians against buying anything from the markets. He also advised the Archbishop to have the Christians boil wheat and to eat only this. In commemoration of the event, the Vesper service of the first Friday of Lent is dedicated to St. Theodore. Hymns of intercession are sung to him and "kolyva," a dish of boiled wheat sweetened with sugar, is blessed in his honor. The hymn is anonymous in the Triodion and attributed to a Theophanes in one manuscript.

Friday in the First Week
at Vespers

Using the apostate Tyrant as his tool,
The enemy, through a cruel plot,
Attempted to defile the people of God
As they purified themselves through
fasting,
5   With food polluted by unclean
sacrifices.
But you defeated his design by a more
skillful plan;
You appeared in a dream to the then
Archbishop,
Revealed the depths of the plot,
And indicated the strange manner of the
undertaking.
10   Therefore we offer to you a sacrifice of
thanksgiving,
We proclaim you as our protector,
And keep a yearly memorial of what
occurred,
And we pray, that we may be kept safe
From the designs of the evil one,
15   Through your intercessions to God,
Great martyr Theodore.

line 1.   The Apostate Emperor Julian (reigned
361-63).
lines 2,14.   The enemy, the evil one; i.e., the
Devil.
line 7.   Archbishop Eudoxius of Constantinople.

Ἁγ. καὶ Μεγάλη Τετάρτη

Κύριε, ἡ ἐν πολλαῖς ἁμαρτίαις
    περιπεσοῦσὰ γυνὴ,
τὴν σὴν αἰσθομένη Θεότητα,
    μυροφόρου ἀναλαβοῦσα τάξιν,
5   ὀδυρομένη μύρον σοι
    πρὸ τοῦ ἐνταφιασμοῦ κομίζει·
Οἴμοι! λέγουσα,
    ὅτι νύξ με συνέχει
    οἶστρος ἀκολασίας.
10 ζοφώδης τε καὶ ἀσέληνος,
    ἔρως τῆς ἁμαρτίας·
δέξαι μου τὰς πηγὰς τῶν δακρύων,
ὁ νεφέλαις στημονίζων
    τῆς θαλάσσης τὸ ὕδωρ·
15 κάμφθητί μοι
    πρὸς τοὺς στεναγμοὺς τῆς καρδίας,

The hymn is known as the penitential hymn on Mary
Magdalene, the sinful woman who washed Christ's feet,
anointed them with myrrh, and wiped them with her long
hair.   It is the highlight of the Vesper service of
Holy Tuesday evening and is sung at the end of the
service.   Manuscript authority attributes both the
words and the melody to Kassia.   However, manuscript
studies show that through the years new arrangements of
the melody were written.   One known arrangement is as
late as the nineteenth century.   The theme of the Holy
Tuesday Vesper service is repentance, forgiveness and
reconciliation with God, and it commemorates the
sinful, penitent woman Mary Magdalene of St. Luke's
gospel (7:36-50).   Her story has been the topic of
countless Lenten sermons and hymns of the Eastern
Church since the fourth century.   Numerous preachers
and hymnographers have elaborated Luke's account.   Many
of these hymns are sung in the Vesper service of Holy
Tuesday, along with three penitential Old Testament
Psalms (37, 50, 142).   Kassia's hymn is the culminating
point of the evening, and its effect on the audience is
one of emotional catharsis.   With emotionally intense
vocabulary, dynamic imagery, and pathos, the sinful
woman's confession, plea for forgiveness, and final
prayer become those of the audience.

Hymn for Holy Wednesday

Lord, the woman fallen
    Into many sins,
Recognizing your Divinity,
    Rises to the status of myrrh-
    bearer,
5   And mourning brings to you myrrh
    Before your burial.
Woe to me, she says,
    For night holds for me
    The ecstasy of intemperance
10   Gloomy and moonless
    A desire for sin.
Accept the springs of my tears,
You who with clouds spread out
    The water of the sea:
15   Bend down to me
    To the lamentations of my heart,

line 4. Mary Magdalene, recognizing Christ's divinity frees herself from sin and rises to the status of the myrrh-bearers, the faithful women followers of Christ who went to his tomb to anoint his body.

line 7. "ohimoi," woe to me, an ancient cry denoting pain and despair.

For a study of the hymn and its place in the tradition of Lenten hymns and penitential psalms, see E. Topping, "The Psalmist, St. Luke and Kassia the Nun." Byzantine Studies, 9 (1982): 199-210. A study of the musical arrangements of the hymn is found in H. J. W. Tillyard, "A Musical Study of the Hymns of Casia." Byzantinische Zeitschrift, 20 (1911): 461-72.

ὁ κλίνας τοὺς οὐρανοὺς
    τῇ ἀφράστῳ σου κενώσει·
καταφιλήσω τοὺς ἀχράντους σου πόδας,
20 ἀποσμήξω τούτους δὲ πάλιν
    τοῖς τῆς κεφαλῆς μου βοστρύχοις·
ὧν ἐν τῷ Παραδείσῳ
    Εὔα τὸν δελινὸν
κρότον τοῖς ὠσὶν ἠχηθεῖσα,
25   τῷ φόβῳ ἐκρύβη·
ἁμαρτιῶν μου τὰ πλήθη
    καὶ κριμάτων σου ἀβύσσους
τίς ἐξιχνιάσει,
    ψυχοσῶστα, Σωτήρ μου;
30 μή με τὴν σὴν δούλην παρίδῃς
    ὁ ἀμέτρητον ἔχων τὸ μέγα ἔλεος.

                    You who made the heavens incline
                        By your ineffable humiliation.
                    I will tenderly kiss your sacred feet,
20   I will wipe them again
                        With the hair of my head;
                    The feet whose sound
                        Eve heard in Paradise
                    In the afternoon,
25   And hid in fear,
                    Who can delineate
                        The multitude of my sins
                    And the depths of your judgment,
                        My Redeemer, savior of souls?
30   Do not disregard me, your servant
                    You, whose mercy is infinite.

     line 18.   In order to save mankind, God inclined
the heavens to earth and stripped himself completely of
his divinity and became man.
     lines 22-25.   After Eve ate of the forbidden
fruit, she fled and hid from God's presence when she
heard His footsteps.   Legend states that at the time
Kassia was composing this hymn, the Emperor Theophilus
paid an unexpected visit to her monastery.   She had
just completed lines 19-21:
                    I will tenderly kiss your sacred feet,
                    I will wipe them again
                        With the hair of my head;
when she heard of the Emperor's unexpected arrival.
She immediately hid.   When the Emperor entered her cell
and saw the unfinished manuscript, he added lines 22-25
                    The feet whose sound
                        Eve heard in Paradise
                    In the afternoon
                        And hid in fear.
Kassia kept Theophilus' addition, and the sentence came
to have a double meaning, Eve's hiding from God and
Kassia's hiding from the Emperor.   However, despite its
popularity among the Greek people to this day, it does
not appear to be true.   There is no evidence of its
origin, nor is it mentioned in any of the Byzantine
chronicles that tell about the brideshow.
     lines 29-31.   The hymn ends with the praise to
God's merciful love and an affirmation of hope that
all, like the sinful woman, will experience God's love
and redeeming mercy.

Τετραώδιον τῷ ἁγίῳ καὶ μεγάλῳ Σαββάτῳ

ΩΔΗ Α΄.

Κύματι θαλάσσης
    τὸν κρύψαντα πάλαι
διώτην τύραννον
    ὑπό γῆν ἔκρυψαν
5   τῶν σεσωσμένων οἱ παῖδες
    ἀλλ' ἡμεῖς ὡς αἱ νεάνιδες
τῷ Κυρίῳ ᾄσωμεν
    ἐνδόξως γάρ δεδόξασται.

* * *

    ῎Αφρον γηραλέε
10   ἀκόρεστε ἅδη
χανών ὑπόδεξαι
    τήν τῶν ἀπάντων ζωήν·
καταπιὼν γὰρ ἐμέσεις
    ἃς προπέπωκας δικαίων ψυχὰς
15   καθελεῖ σε Κύριος
    ὅτι δεδόξασται.

* * *

᾿Ιησοῦ Θεέ μου
    ὑμνῶ σου τὰ πάθη·
ἑκὼν γὰρ τέθνηκας
20   ὑπέρ τῆς πάντων ζωῆς
καὶ ἐν σινδόνι καὶ σμύρνη
    κηδευθῆναι κατηξίωσας
τὴν ταφήν δοξάζω σου
    ὑμνῶ σου καὶ τὴν ἔγερσιν.

    The canon celebrates Christ's burial, His descent into hell and His victory over death, and anticipates his rising again, bringing new life and recreating the world. It is considered by the Eastern Church one of the most beautiful and important hymns of Holy Week for the beauty of its words, poetic feeling and melody. Tradition attributes both the words and melody to Kassia, but only the original "heirmoi" or the first stanza of every ode has been incorporated into the official Lenten book, the <u>Triodion</u>. According to

Tetraodion for Holy Saturday

Ode One

He who once
    Hid the pursuing tyrant
In the waves of the sea,
    Was hidden beneath the earth
5   By the children of those he had saved.
    But let us, as the maidens,
Sing unto the Lord,
    For he is greatly glorified.

* * *

Senseless, old,
10   Insatiable, gaping
Hell, receive
    The life of all mankind.
For you will be sick devouring
    The souls of the righteous that you
    had swallowed down;
15   The Lord will strike you down
    Because He is glorified.

* * *

Christ, my God,
    I sing in praise of your Passion,
For you willingly died
20   On behalf of everyone's life
And condescended to be buried
    In a sheet and with myrrh;
I glorify your burial
    And I offer praise to your raising.

Theodoros Podromos, who in the twelfth century wrote
commentaries on the hymns of some of the Church's more
famous hymnographers, the Church felt that a hymn for
a major religious holiday could not be attributed to a
woman. Therefore, the canon was attributed to a male
hymnographer, Cosmas (c.685-750), Bishop of Maiouma in
Phoenicia. Early in the tenth century, at the command
of the Emperor Leo IV, the Wise (886-912), Bishop
Marcus of Hydrous, Italy composed five additional odes

ΩΔΗ Γ΄.

25   Σὲ τὸν ἐπὶ ὑδάτων
           κρεμάσαντα πᾶσαν τὴν γῆν ἀσχέτως
      ἡ κτίσις κατιδοῦσα
           ἐν τῷ κρανίῳ κρεμάμενον
      θάμβει πολλῷ συνείχετο
30   οὐκ ἔστιν ἅγιος
      πλήν σου, Κύριε, κραυγάζουσα.

                    * * *

           Ἔθεντό σε ἐν λάκκῳ,
      μακρόθυμε σωτήρ, οἱ Ἰουδαῖοι
           καὶ ἐν σκιᾷ θανάτου
35   τὸν ἐν νεκροῖς ἐλεύθερον
           τὸν καὶ μοχλοὺς συντρίψαντα
      τοῦ ᾄδου, δέσποτα,
           τοὺς θανόντας ἐγείραντα.

                    * * *

           Πᾶσι τοῖς ἐν ἀλύτοις
40   σειραῖς τοῦ ᾄδου πεπεδημένοις
      ὁ Κύριος ἐβόα
           οἱ ἐν δεσμοῖς ἐξέλθετε
      οἱ ἐν τῷ σκότει λύεσθε
           ὁ βασιλεὺς ἡμῶν
45   τοὺς ἐν γῇ λυτρούμενος.

---

to the canon. He also completely altered the original
odes and retained only the "heirmoi" of each ode and
the melody. The canon exists in its altered form in
the <u>Triodion</u>. Kassia's original hymn, transcribed and
translated here, is found in only two early manuscripts
in the library of Mt. Athos.

Ode Three

25   When the creation observed you
                Hanging on Golgotha,
            Who without hindrance hung the whole
                earth
                Upon the waters,
            It was filled with great astonishment
30   And cried out, "There is no one
                holy
            Except you, O Lord."

* * *

                The Jews placed you in a pit
            And in the shadow of Death,
                O long-suffering Savior,
35   The free one among the dead,
                The one who crushed the barriers
            Of hell, O master,
                Raising those who had died.

* * *

            To all those shackled
40   With the indestructible chains of
                hell
            The Lord shouted:
                "Those in bondage burst forth,
            Those in darkness be free."
                Our King is delivering
45   Those in the earth.

line 35. the free one; i.e., the immortal.

ΩΔΗ Δ'.

Τὴν ἐν σταυρῷ σου θείαν κένωσιν
    προορῶν Ἀββοκοὺμ
ἐξεστηκὼς ἐβόα
    σὺ δυναστῶν δείκοψας
50   Κράτος, ἀγαθέ,
    ὁμιλῶν τοῖς ἐν ᾅδῃ
ὡς παντοδύναμος.

* * *

Ὁ τὴν ζωὴν πηγάζων Κύριος
    γεγονὼς συμπαθῶς
55   ἐν τοῖς ὑποχθονίοις
    τὸ φῶς τὸ τῆς θεότητος
ἔλαμψας θνητοῖς
    καθελὼν τὴν τοῦ ᾅδου
ζοφώδη δύναμιν.

* * *

60   Νενικημένος ὁ πανδόλιος
    ἑαυτὸν καθορῶν
ἐχθρὸς τῇ καταβάσει
    σοῦ τῇ εἰς ᾅδου, δέσποτα,
τὸ κράτος μου βοᾷ
65   κατεπόθη καὶ πᾶσα
ἡ δυναστεία μου.

Ode Four

Habakkuk foreseeing
    Your divine self-emptying upon the
    cross,
Cried out in amazement:
    "You have cut short the strength
50   Of the powerful, O benevolent one,
    Preaching to those in hell
As almighty."

* * *

The Lord who is the source of life
    Became compassionate
55   To those under the earth,
    Shone the light
Of his divinity to mortals
    Striking down
The dark power of hell.

* * *

60   The all-deceitful enemy,
    Perceiving himself conquered
By your descent
    Into hell, O Master,
Cries out: "My power
65   And all my rule
Has been swallowed up."

lines 49-52.   Habakkuk 3:1-19.

ΩΔΗ Ε'.

Θεοφανείας σου Χριστέ,
    τῆς πρὸς ἡμᾶς συμπαθῶς γενομένης
Ἡσαίας φῶς ἰδὼν ἀνέσπερον
70   ἐκ νυκτὸς ὀρθρίσας ἐκραύγαζεν·
ἀναστήσονται οἱ νεκροὶ
    καὶ ἐγερθήσονται οἱ ἐν τοῖς
    μνημείοις
καὶ πάντες οἱ ἐν τῇ γῇ
    αγαλλιάσονται.

                    * * *

75   Τοῦ ψυχοφθόρου τὴν ὀφρύν
          διὰ σταυροῦ νεκρωθείς, εὐεργέτα,
    καταβὰς εἰς ἄδου δὲ συνέτριψας
          τοὺς αὐτοῦ μοχλοὺς καὶ ἀνέστησας
    τὸν προπάτορα ὡς Θεὸς
80   καὶ τῇ νεκρώσει σου τοῖς πιστοῖς
          παρέσχες
    εἰρήνην καὶ τὴν ζωὴν
          καὶ ἀγαλλίασιν.

                    * * *

    Τοῖς ἐν τῷ ἄδῃ συνοικῶν
          ὁ τὴν ζωὴν τοῖς βροτοῖς ἀναβλύσας
85   τοῖς ἐν σκότει ἔλεγες ἐξέλθετε
          καὶ τοῖς ἐν δεσμοῖς ἀπολύθετε·
    εἰς ὤλεσιν τοῦ ἐχθροῦ
          καὶ εἰς ἀνάστασιν τῶν προτεθνηκότων
    ἐλήλυθα πρὸς ζωὴν
90   ἀνακαλούμενος.

Ode Five

Isaiah, as he watched by night,
    beheld the light that knows no
    evening,
Your divine manifestation, O Christ,
70   That came to pass because of your
      compassion for us and cried
      out:
"The dead shall arise
    And they that are in the tomb shall
    be raised,
And all those on the earth,
    Shall rejoice exceedingly."

            * * *

75 By means of the cross, O benefactor.
    You mortified the pride of the soul
    destroyer
Descending into hell, you crushed
    Its barriers and as God
Raised the forefather,
80   And by your death granted to the
    faithful
Peace and life
    And exultation.

            * * *

You who breathed life into mortals
    Lived with those in hell
85 To those in darkness you told to come
    out
    And to those in bonds to be
    released,
To the destruction of the enemy;
    And when you called those who had
    died before
To rise up
90   I came to life.

lines 71-74. Isaiah 26:19.
line 79. Adam.

ΚΑΝΩΝ ΑΝΑΠΑΥΣΙΜΟΣ ΕΙΣ ΚΟΙΜΗΣΙΝ.

ΩΔΗ Α΄.

Ὕψος καὶ βάθος τίς ἐκφράσαι δύναται
τῆς σῆς σοφίας Χριστέ,
καὶ τῆς δυνάμεώς σου
τὸ ἄπειρον πέλαγος,
5   πῶς ἐκ μὴ ὄντων ἅπαντα
τῇ βουλῇ καὶ τῷ λόγῳ
τῷ σῷ παρήγαγες, δέσποτα;
ὅθεν σε ἀπαύστως δοξάζωμεν.

Πέπονθεν πρὶν ἐπιβουλὴν τὸ πλάσμα σου
10   ἐν τῇ Ἐδέμ, λυτρωτά,
καὶ τὸ Εἰς γῆν αὖθις
ἀπελεύσει ἤκουσεν
ὡς ἐκ τῆς γῆς γενόμενον·
οὐκ ἐνέγκας πλὴν τοῦτο
15   ὑπὸ τοῦ Ἅιδου κρατούμενον
ἦλθες, ὁ σωτήρ μου, καὶ ἔσωσας.

Ἐπὶ τῆς γῆς ὁ ἐν ὑψίστοις γέγονας
σαρκὸς θνητῆς μετασχών,
ἵνα θνητοὺς πάντας,
20   ἀφθαρσίας δέσποτα,
καὶ εἰς τὴν πρὶν ἀπάθειαν
μεταστήσας ζωώσῃς·
διὸ καὶ νῦν, οὓς μετέστησας,
τάξον ἐν σκηναῖς τῶν δικαίων σου.

Canon for the Dead

This canon, acknowledged to be a genuine work of Kassia, was written to be sung in the monastery cemetery during the weekly memorial service for those buried there held every Saturday. It is a typical Eastern Christian hymn of intercession for the dead, with the exception of the last stanza or Theotokion, lines 245-52. Here Kassia invokes Christ to protect and guide the "faithful monarch." In composition, the hymn follows the traditional form of the canon. It contains eight odes numbered one and three to nine, see p. xvi above. Each ode has three troparia or stanzas

Ode One

Christ, who is able to recount
the height and depth of your wisdom
and the infinite greatness
of your power,
5   how by your will and word
created everything
out of nothing, oh Lord?
for which we unceasingly praise you.

Meanwhile your creation suffered the
        intrigue
10   in Eden, Savior,
and heard that having come
from earth
it will again return to earth;
but not being able to endure
15   its being held by death,
you came, oh my Savior, and saved it.

The one dwelling on high came to earth
taking a mortal body,
so that, lord of immortality,
20   you could give life
to all mortals and
return them to the former sinless state;
therefore, now those whom you have
        returned
assign them to the place of your
        righteous ones.

line 9. a creation, referring to Adam and Eve.
lines 11-13. Cf. Gen. 3:19.

---

and ends with a Theotokion, a troparion in honor of the
Theotokos or Mother of God.
    This is Kassia's longest work, 32 stanzas, 252
lines, and the least original and impressive.   It
follows   the   hymnographical   tradition   of   her
contemporary ecclesiastical poets.   Thus,   it   is
lengthy, repetitive, and heavily dependent on Biblical
phraseology.   Moreover,   only   two   of   the   hymn's
Theotokia are original; the one at the end of ode five
and at the end of ode nine. The others, with the

Θεοτοκίον

25   Δεδοξασμένα περὶ σοῦ λελάληται
      ἐν γενεαῖς γενεῶν,
      ἡ τὸν θεὸν λόγον
      ἐν γαστρὶ χωρέσασα,
      ἀγνὴ δὲ διαμείνασα,
30   Θετοτόκε Μαρία·
      διὸ πρεσβείαις σου λύτρωσαι
      τοὺς προκοιμηθέντας τῆς κρίσεως.

                    ΩΔΗ Γ'.

      Ὅταν ἐλεύσῃ, ὁ θεός,
      ἐπὶ τῆς γῆς μετὰ δόξης
35   καὶ ὡς μέλλεις τὰ πρακτέα ἑκάστου
      μέχρι λόγου παριστᾶν
      ἀργοῦ τε ἐννοίας ψιλῆς,
      τῶν μεταστάντων φεῖσαι
      καὶ ῥῦσαι τούτους τῆς κρίσεως.

40   Νεκρῶν ἐν τρόμῳ καὶ σπουδῇ
      τῶν τάφων ἀποτρεχόντων
      καὶ τῆς σάλπιγγος ἠχούσης, σωτήρ μου,
      καὶ ἀγγέλων φοβερῶν
      σου προστρεχόντων, κύριε,
45   τῶν μεταστάντων φεῖσαι
      καὶ τάξον τούτους ἐν χώρᾳ ζωῆς.

      Τοῦ οὐρανοῦ τε καὶ τῆς γῆς
      σαλευομένων, οἰκτίρμων,
      καὶ στοιχείων λυομένων ἐν φόβῳ
50   τοὺς οἰκέτας σου φαιδρῶς
      πρὸς ὑπάντησιν ποίησον,
      ὅτι ἐκτός σου ἄλλον,
      δέσποτα, θεὸν οὐκ ἔγνωσαν.

exception of a few minor word changes, can be traced to
various other religious works found throughout the
Church's liturgical books. The canon for the dead is
Kassia's only religious work that is not found in the
ecclesiastical books of the Eastern Church. It is
found in an eleventh-century manuscript from Grotta
Ferrata and was first studied and published by K.
Krumbacher, see K. Krumbacher, _Kasia_, p.323ff.

Theotokion

25   Glorious things have been said about you
from generation to generation,
the one who contained in her womb
the Divine Logos,
but remaining pure,
30   Mary, Mother of God;
therefore   redeem   through   your
     intercession
those who have died before the judgment.

Ode Three

God, when you return
to earth with Glory
35   and as you are about to present
the deeds of each to the last,
idle word and simple thought,
have consideration for the departed
and deliver them from judgment.

40   My savior, when the dead in fear and
     haste
run from the graves
and from the sound of the trumpet
and when your fearful angels
run toward them, lord,
45   have consideration for the departed
and place them in a land of eternal
     life.

When the earth and sky
are tottering, merciful one,
and when the foundations are crumbling
     in fear,
50   joyously prepare to meet
your servants,
because except for you, master,
they have not known another god.

Θεοτοκίον

Τῶν Χερουβὶμ καὶ Σεραφὶμ
55   ἐδείχθης ὑψηλοτέρα,
Θεοτόκε σὺ γὰρ μόνη ἐδέξω
τὸν ἀχώρητον θεὸν
ἐν σῇ γαστρὶ χωρήσασα·
διὸ αὐτὸν δυσώπει,
60   κρίσεως ῥῦσαι τοὺς δούλους σου.

ΩΔΗ Δ'.

Ὁ τῆς ζωῆς κύριος καὶ τοῦ θανάτου,
        Χριστέ,
ὁ σωμάτων καὶ ψυχῶν ταμίας τε,
ὅταν φρικτῶς μέλλῃς ἐπὶ γῆς
μετὰ τῶν ἀγγέλων τῶν σῶν ἐν δόξῃ
        ἐλεύσεσθαι
65   καὶ κρῖναι πᾶσαν κτίσιν,
τοὺς πρὸς σὲ μεταστάντας
δεξιοῖς σου προβάτοις κατάταξον.

Νεῦσον, Χριστὲ κύριε, πρὸς ἱκεσίαν ἡμῶν
καὶ τῆς ἄνω θείας κληρουχίας σου
70   τοὺς ἐξ ἡμῶν πίστει τῇ εἰς σὲ
προκεκοιμημένους ἀξίωσον ὡς φιλάνθρωπος
φωνῆς τέ σου ἀκοῦσαι
τῆς γλυκείας καλούσης
εἰς ἀνάπαυσιν τούτους, δεόμεθα.

75   Ἅπας βροτὸς οἴχεται· γῆ γάρ ἐστιν καὶ
        σποδός
σὺ δὲ μόνος μένεις εἰς αἰῶνας, Χριστέ,
ἀνελλιπής μένεις γὰρ θεός·
διό σοι βοῶμεν Τῆς σῆς ἀλήκτου ἀξίωσον
χαρᾶς τοὺς σοὺς οἰκέτας
80   τοῦ βοᾶν εὐχαρίστως·
Τῇ δυνάμει σου δόξα, φιλάνθρωπε.

Theotokion

You have shown yourself to be loftier
55   than the Seraphim and Cherubim,
Mother of God; for you alone received
the infinite God
containing him in your womb;
therefore entreat him,
60   to deliver your servants from judgment.

Ode Four

Christ, lord of life and death,
and dispenser of bodies and souls,
when, awesomely, you intend to return
to earth in glory along with your angels
65   and to judge all creation,
place those who have turned to you
with the sheep on your right hand.

Christ, lord, incline toward our
    supplication,
and as one who is benevolent
70   consider worthy of your divine
    inheritance above
those of us who having already fallen
    asleep in death
were faithful to you while here,
and, we implore, that they hear
your sweet voice inviting them to
    eternal rest.
75   Every mortal perishes; for it is earth
    and ashes,
but you alone, Christ, remain perfect
through the ages; for you remain God;
therefore we cry out to you: consider
    worthy
of your unending joy your servants
80   who gratefully celebrate you.
Glory to your power, oh benevolent one.

line 67.   sheep, a term used by Christians to
refer to the faithful Christians.

Θεοτοκίον.

Σὺ τῶν πιστῶν καύχημα πέλεις, ἀνύμφευτε,
σὺ προστάτις, σὺ καὶ καταφύγιον,
χριστιανῶν τεῖχος καὶ λιμήν·
85   πρὸς γὰρ τὸν υἱόν σου ἐντεύξεις φέρεις,
      πανάμωμε·
αὐτὸν καὶ νῦν δυσώπει,
τοὺς προτελειωθέντας
τῆς κολάσεως ῥύσασθαι, πάναγνε.

ΩΔΗ Ε'.

Μετὰ δόξης, οἰκτίρμων, ὅταν ἥξεις τοῦ
      κρῖναι
90   δικαίως πᾶσαν (τὴν) γῆν
καὶ διαχωρίσεις
ἐξ ἀδίκων δικαίους, ὡς γέγραπται,
δεξιοῖς προβάτοις
τοὺς ἐξ ἡμῶν συναριθμήσας
95   μεταστάντας, οἰκίρμων, ἀνάπαυσον.

Ἀτελεύτητος ὄντως τοῖς ἀσώτως ζήσασιν
ἔστιν ἡ κόλασις,
ὁ βρυγμὸς καὶ σκώληξ
καὶ κλαυθμὸς ἀπαράκλητος, κύριε,
100   καὶ τὸ πῦρ ἐκεῖνο
τὸ ἀφεγγές, τὸ σκότος πάλιν,
ἐξ ὧν ῥῦσαι τοὺς δούλους σου,
      εὔσπλαγχνε.

Χαρᾶς τῆς ἀπεράντου καὶ ἀφθόρου τρυφῆς
      σου,
Χριστέ, σωτὴρ ἡμῶν,
105   τοὺς προκοιμηθέντας
καταξίωσον ὡς εὐδιάλλακτος
τῶν ἐν βίῳ πάντων
ἀμνημονῶν ἀμαρτημάτων·
οὐ γὰρ ἔσχον ἐκτός σου θεόν ἀγαθέ.

Theotokion

You are the pride of the faithful,
  unwedded virgin,
you are the advocate, the refuge
of Christians, their rampart and haven;
85 for you offer to your son intercessions,
  undefiled one;
convince him now, all pure one,
to save from punishment
those who have already died.

Ode Five

Merciful one, when you come with glory
90 to justly judge all the earth
and you separate
the righteous from the unrighteous, as
  it is written,
give rest, merciful one,
to those of us who have departed
95 and include us among the sheep on your
  right.
Divine punishment is truly endless
for those who live dissolutely,
Lord, there is the gnashing of teeth,
  worms
comfortless weeping
100 and that fire
without light, and back to darkness,
deliver your servants from this,
  compassionate one.

Christ, our savior,
as one who is forgiving, consider
105 those who have already fallen asleep in
  death,
worthy of your boundless joy and eternal
  bliss,
being unmindful of all the
  transgressions
during their lifetime;
for they had no other god but you, holy
  one.

Θετοκίον.

110   Ἐν δυσὶ τελείαις ἕνα σε γινώσκομεν
       φύσεσι κύριον,
       ἐνεργείαις ἄμφω
       καὶ θελήσεσιν ὄντα ἀσύγχυτον,
       τὸν υἱὸν τοῦ θεοῦ,
115   ἐκ γυναικὶς λαβόντα σάρκα,
       ἧς τὴν θέαν τιμῶμεν τοῖς πίναξιν.

ΩΔΗ ΣΤ'.

       Ῥευστοὶ τεχθέντες βροτοὶ
       ἄρευστοι ἀναστησόμεθα
       καθὼς ἐξ ὕπνου, φησὶν
120   ὡς Παῦλος ὁ πάνσοφος,
       βροντώσης τῆς σάλπιγγος·
       ἀλλὰ τότε ῥῦσαι
       κατακρίσεως τοὺς δούλους σου.

       Ἱλάσθητι ὁ θεὸς
125   τοῖς δούλους σου ἐν ἡμέρᾳ ὀργῆς,
       ὅταν γυμνοὶ ἐπὶ σοῦ
       παραστῆναι μέλλωσιν·
       τούτους, σῶτερ, λύτρωσαι
       τῆς φωνῆς ἐκείνης
130   τῆς εἰς πῦρ ἀποπεμπούσης, θεέ.

       Συγκλείσεις ὅτε, Χριστέ,
       ἐνταῦθα βίον καὶ πρᾶξιν ἡμῶν
       καὶ στήσεις πάντων ἡμῶν
       τῶν ἔργων ἀξέτασιν,
135   μὴ ἐλέγξῃς, κύριε,
       ὧνπερ προσελάβου,
       ἀναμάρτητε, τὰ πταίσματα.

Theotokion

110 We acknowledge you one lord
in two complete natures,
both in will and activity,
the son of God,
115 who received flesh from a woman
whose countenance we honor in icons.

Ode Six

Created as changeable mortals
we will arise incorruptible
as from sleep, as the
120 all-wise Paul said,
from the thundering of the trumpet;
but at that time deliver
your servants from judgment.

God be merciful
125 to your servants on the day of wrath,
when we must stand
naked before you;
deliver them, savior,
from the voice
130 that banishes one to the fire, oh God.

Christ, when you conclude
our lives and deeds here on earth
and begin the scrutiny
of all our deeds,
135 don't cross examine, lord,
the transgressions of those
you have already received.

line 119. Rom. 13:11. The reference here is to
the resurrection of the dead on Judgment Day.

Θεοτοκίον.

'Ρυσθείημεν τῶν δεινῶν
πταισμάτων ταῖς ἱκεσίαις σου,
140   θεογεννήτωρ ἁγνή,
καὶ τύχοιμεν, πάναγνε,
τῆς θείας ἐλλάμψεως
τοῦ ἐκ σοῦ ἀφράστως
σαρκωθέντος υἱοῦ τοῦ θεοῦ.

ΩΔΗ Ζ'.

145   Τὸ ἄστεκτον, κύριε,
τῆς σῆς φρικώδους
ἐπαγωγῆς ἐννοῶν,
ὅπως μέλλεις δικαίως
κατὰ <τὰ> ἔργα κρῖναι ἑκάστου ἡμῶν,
150   στένων βοῶ σοι·
Τῶν δούλων σου πάριδε
τὰ ἐν ἀγνοίᾳ, σωτήρ,
καὶ γνώσει πταίσματα.

'Ως ἔχων, μακρόθυμε,
155   φιλανθρωπίας
ἄπλετον πέλαγος,
τῶν πρὸς σὲ μεταστάντων
μὴ στήσῃς ὅλως τὰ παραπτώματα
ἐν τῇ ἐτάσει
160   αὐτῶν κατὰ πρόσωπον,
ἀλλὰ συγχώρησον καὶ
σῶσον τούτους, Χριστέ.

Κριτὰ δικαιότατε,
ὅτε τὰς πράξεις
165   ζυγοστατήσεις ἡμῶν,
μὴ δικάσῃς δικαίως,
ἀλλὰ νικήσοι ἡ ἀγαθότης σου
ὑπερσταθμῶσα
τὴν πλάστιγγα, κύριε,
170   ἥνπερ τὰ φαῦλα, σωτήρ,
ἔργα βαρύνουσιν.

Theotokion

140

Undefiled mother of God,
may we be delivered from our
grievous transgressions by your prayers,
and may we dwell, all pure one,
in the divine glory
of the Son of God
who ineffably took flesh from you.

Ode Seven

145

Lord, understanding the relentlessness
of your awe-inspiring manner
of how you intend to judge
justly according to each
of our deeds.

150

I cry out to you in deep sorrow.
Savior, overlook the transgressions
of your servants
done in ignorance and knowingly.

155

Long-suffering one,
since you have a boundless
measure of love for mankind,
during the trial of those who have
    already departed to you,
don't place all their transgressions

160

before them,
but forgive them
and save them, oh Christ.

Most impartial judge,
when you weigh

165

our deeds,
don't judge with reason,
but let your goodness prevail
and add weight
to the scale, lord,

170

when the evil deeds
tip it the other way.

Θεοτοκίον.

Θαυμάτων ἐπέκεινα
τὸ μέγα θαῦμα
τῆς σῆς κυήσεως·
175   διὰ τοῦτο βοῶμεν·
      Ἁγνὴ παρθένε, θεογεννήτρια,
τὰ σὰ ἐλέη
ἐμοὶ θαυμάστωσον
καὶ τῆς μελλούσης ὀργῆς
180   ῥῦσαι καὶ σῶσόν με.

ΩΔΗ Η'.

Ἀπαγωγῆς, φιλάνθρωπε,
τοῦ προσώπου σου λύτρωσαι
καὶ τῆς φοβερᾶς σου ἀπειλῆς τοὺς δούλους
      σου
καὶ τούτους ἀξίωσον
185   τοῦ φωτισμοῦ τῆς γνώσεως
καὶ τῆς συνουσίας σου βοᾶν σοι ἀπαύστως·
Οἱ παῖδες εὐλογεῖτε
<ἱερεῖς ἀνυμνεῖτε>
      ....
190   ....

Σοῦ ὁ θυμός, φιλάνθρωπε,
ἐκχυθήτω, δεόμεθα,
ἐπι τοὺς ἐν σοὶ μὴ ἠλπικότας ὅλως,
      Χριστέ,
ὁ οἶκτος δὲ ἅμα τε
195   καὶ ἡ πλουσία χάρις σου
ἐπὶ τοὺς εἰς σὲ πεπιστευκότας δοθήτω.
λαός σου γὰρ καὶ ποίμνη
καὶ πρόβατα νομῆς σου·
καὶ σὲ ὑπερυψοῦμεν
200   εἰς πάντας <τοὺς αἰῶνας>.

Theotokion

Beyond all wonders
in the great miracle
of your conception;

175   therefore we cry out to you.
           Undefiled virgin, god-bearer,
           have mercy on the things that concern
               you,
           marveled by me,
           and deliver me and
180   save me from the future wrath.

Ode Eight

Merciful one, save your servants
from being led away from your presence
and from the threatening circumstances
we unceasingly cry out to you
185   to make them worthy
           of the light of knowledge
           Children bless (the Lord)
           (priests praise him in song)
           ....
190   ....

Benevolent one, we pray that
your wrath is poured out
upon those who did not trust in you,
               Christ,
but grant to those who believed in you
195   compassion along with
           your infinite grace.
           For they are your people and flock
           and the sheep of your pasture,
           and we exalt you above all
200   forever.

line 186. cf. II Cor. 4:6.

lines 189-90. There is a lacuna of two lines in the manuscript.

Σὺ τὸ φρικτὸν ποτήριον
τοῦ ἀκράτου κεράσματος
τὸ ἐν τῇ χειρί σου, λυτρωτά, δεόμεθα,
πραΰτητι σύμμιξον
205   καὶ τῆς τρυγίας τούτους τοὺς σοὺς
λύτρωσαι οἰκέτας, οὓς ἐκ γῆς προσελάβου,
καὶ τάξον ἐν τῇ χώρᾳ
τῶν πραέων, οἰκτίρμων,
ὑμνεῖν καὶ εὐλογεῖν σε
210   εἰς πάντας τοὺς αἰῶνας.

                    Θεοτοκίον.

'Ικετικῶς βοῶμέν σοι,
θεοτόκε πανύμνητε,
μετὰ τῶν ἀπείρων νοερῶν δυνάμεων,
μαρτύρων ὀσίων τε
215   καὶ ἀποστόλων καὶ προφητῶν
ποίησον πρεσβείαν ὑπὲρ τῶν μεταστάντων.
χορεύειν σὺν ἀγγέλοις,
ψάλλειν δὲ τῷ υἱῷ σου·
Λαός ὑπ <ερυψοῦτε
220   εἰς πάντας τοὺς αἰῶνας>.

                    We pray, oh Deliverer
                    that you mix the terrible cup
                    of unmixed drink in your hand
                    with gentleness
205   and save those of your servants,
                    whom you have already taken from the
                        earth,
                    from this sediment and place them
                    in the land of the meek, merciful one,
                    to praise and bless you
210   forever.

                        Theotokion

                    Humbly we cry out to you,
                    mother of God worthy of all praise,
                    with the help of the infinite spiritual
                        powers,
                    the holy martyrs
215   and the apostles and prophets
                    intercede on behalf of the departed,
                    to take part in the chorus with the
                        angels,
                    and sing psalms to your son.
                    People, magnify the Lord
220   forever.

lines 202-03.   The cup of wine of the wrath of
God.   Cf. Rev. 14:10.

ΩΔΗ Θ'.

Ἰστῶντός σου, οἰκτίρμων, τὸ φοβερὸν
δικαστήριον, ὅτε ἡ γῆ καὶ ὑγρὰ
φόβῳ πολλῷ κτήνη καὶ θηρία καὶ ἑρπετὰ
καὶ τοὺς νεκροὺς τοὺς ἑαυτῶν
225   (ἐν) τρόμῳ (σου, σῶτερ) ἀποπέμπουσιν
πρὸς τὴν σὴν
ὑπάντησιν σπουδαίως,
τοὺς πίστει μεταστάντας
μὴ καταισχύνῃς, ὑπεράγαθε.

Ἀείμνηστοι πατέρες καὶ ἀδελφοί,
230   συγγενε-ις τε καὶ φίλοι καὶ σύμψυχοί
<μου>,
οἱ τὴν ὁδὸν προκαταλαβόντες τὴν φοβεράν,
ἀντὶ μερίδος δέξασθε
δῶρον τὸ ἐφέμνιον παρ' ἐμοῦ·
καὶ ὅσοι παρρησίας
235   ἐτύχετε, τὸν κτίστην
ὑπὲρ ἐμοῦ καθικετεύσατε.

Σωτὴρ ἀπελισμένων σου τὴν φρικτήν,
ὥσπερ εἶπας, θυσίαν τελοῦντες φρικτῶς
καὶ τὴν φρικτὴν ἐκούσιον ἀγγέλλοντες
(τὴν) σφαγὴν
240   εἰς ἱκεσίαν ἅπαντες
ταύτην σοι προσφέρωμεν ἐκτενῶς
ὑπὲρ τῶν μεταστάντων
πρὸς σὲ τὸν ζωοδότην,
οὓς σὺν ἁγίοις σου ἀνάπαυσον.

Θεοτοκίον.

245   Υἱὲ θεοῦ καὶ λόγε μονογενῆ
τὸν πιστὸν βασιλέα στεφάνωσον
τῇ πανσθενεῖ, δέσποτα, χειρί σου, ὡς
ἀγαθός·
καὶ δυσμενῶν τὸ κράτος νῦν
ὄλεσον τῷ ὅπλῳ τῷ τοῦ στρατοῦ
250   διὰ τῆς Θεοτόκου
καὶ σῶσον τὸν λαόν σου
ἐν τῇ ἀγήρῳ βασιλείᾳ σου.

Ode Nine

Merciful one, when you establish your
    formidable
court of justice, when the earth and
    sea,
flocks and herds, wild beasts and
    animals,
in great awe send their dead
225   trembling with fear of you to meet
you with haste,
don't find the departed faithful
unworthy, you who are beyond goodness.

Ever-remembered fathers, brothers, and
    sisters,
230   relatives, friends, and my soul-mates,
who have already taken the terrible
    road,
instead of a contribution accept
a gift of this hymn by me
and as many of you are fortunate
235   to gain the bliss of heaven, earnestly
entreat the creator on my behalf.

Savior of the desperate, trembling with
    fear
we celebrate your terrible sacrifice,
as you called it, and we proclaim your
240   terrible and voluntary death in a
    universal prayer.
This we offer fervently to you
on behalf of those who have departed,
to you the giver of life,
give them rest among your saints.

Theotokion

245   Son of God and only begotten Word
crown the faithful King
with your all mighty hand, kind Lord,
and then with the army assisted
by the Mother of God,
250   destroy the strength of the enemy
and save your people
in your eternal Kingdom.

EPIGRAMS AND GNOMIC VERSES

Φιλία

Δύο φιλούντων τὴν ἐν Χριστῷ φιλίαν
ἰσασμὸς οὐκ ἔνεστιν, ἀλλ' ἔρις μᾶλλον.

Φίλῳ φιλοῦντι χαρίζου τὸ φιλεῖσθαι,
τῷ δ' ἀγνώμονι εἰς κενὸν τὸ φιλεῖθαι.

5   Μέγα τὸ μικρόν, ἂν ὁ φίλος εὐγνώμων·
τῷ δ' ἀχαρίστῳ σμικρότατον τὸ μέγα.

Εἰ θέλεις πάντως καὶ φιλεῖν καὶ
        φιλεῖσθαι,
τῶν ψιθυριστῶν καὶ φθονερῶν ἀπέχου.

Φίλος ἐν λύπαις συνὼν τοῖς φιλεστάτοις
10   ὕφεσιν εὗρε τῶν σφοδρῶν ἀλγηδόνων.

Φρόνιμον φίλον ὡς χρυσὸν κόλπῳ βάλλε,
τὸν δ' αὖ γε μωρὸν φεῦγε καθάπερ ὄφιν.

Φίλον φιλητὸς φιλοῦντα συναντήσας
γέγηθε λαμπρῶς ὥσπερ ὄγκον εὑρὼν
        χρυσίου.

Friendship

In a friendship that is [not] founded
in Christ
Harmony is not possible, but rather
strife.

Give freely of friendship to a loving
friend,
but to an ungrateful one, friendship
is vain.

5   A little is the most, if the friend is
grateful,
but to the ungrateful the most is the
least.

If you want to love and to be loved
completely,
keep away from slanderers and the
envious.

A friend sharing his sufferings with
his dearest friends
10   finds relaxation from extreme
distress.

Take an understanding friend to your
bosom as you would gold,
but avoid the foolish one just as you
would a serpent.

One worthy of friendship when he meets
a loving friend
vigorously rejoices as if he found a
large sum of money.

line 1. The word μή– [not] is not found in K.
Krumbacher's transcription of the fifteenth-century
manuscript where these gnomic verses are found.
However, the statement does not make sense without
it. The word was left out either by the scribe of
the manuscript or in transcription.

lines 9-10. ἀλγηδόνων, a term meaning both
mental and physical suffering or distress.

15   Φίλος δ' ὑψωθεὶς συνυψώσει τοὺς
          φίλους.

          Κρεῖσσον δὲ πάντως καὶ χρυσοῦ καὶ
             μαργάρων
          ἑσμὸς φιλούντων πρὸς φιλοῦντας
             γνησίως.

          Φραγμὸς πέφυκεν ἡ τῶν φίλων ἀγάπη.

          Πλοῦτος δ' ἄχρηστος, ἐὰν μὴ φίλον ἔχῃ.

20   Φίλος τὸν φίλον καὶ χώρα χώραν σῴζει.

          Φίλων φιλούντων ἐν λύπαις ὁμιλίαι
          ἡδύτεραι μέλιτος παντὸς καὶ ὄψου.

          Φίλον γνήσιον δ' ἡ περίστασις δείξει·
          οὐ γὰρ ἀποστήσεται τοῦ φιλουμένου.

25   Φίλος λεγέσθω ὁ φιλῶν ἄνευ δόλου,
          ὁ δ' σὺν δόλῳ οὐ φίλος, ἀλλ' ἐχθρός
          σοι.

          Ὥσπερ σκοτεινὸς οἶκος οὐκ ἔχει
             τέρψιν,
          οὕτως πέφυκεν ὁ πλοῦτος ἄνευ φίλων.

15   A friend who becomes exalted will
                elevate his friends along with
                him.

            Far more valuable than gold and a
                cluster of pearls
            are friends, above all those who are
                genuinely friends.

            The love of friends forms a protective
                fence.

            Wealth is useless if one does not
                have a friend.

20   A friend saves a friend and a place
                saves a place.

            The company of friends when friends
                are in distress
            is sweeter than all the honey and
                choice food.

            A crisis will reveal a true friend;
            for he will not desert the one who is
                his friend.

25   Regard as a friend one who loves
                without cunning,
            on the other hand one who is cunning
                is not a friend but an enemy.

            Wealth without friends
            is a dark dwelling place in which
                there is no joy.

Μέτρον Ἰκασίας διὰ στίχων ἰάμβων.

Μισῶ

Μισῶ φονέα κρίνοντα τὸν θυμώδη.
Μισῶ τὸν μιοχόν, ὅταν κρίνῃ τὸν
πόρνον.
Μισῶ κελεφὸν τὸν λεπρὸν ἐξωθοῦντα.
Μισῶ τὸν μωρὸν φιλοσοφεῖν δοκοῦντα.
5   Μισῶ δικαστὴν προσέχοντα προσώποις.
Μισῶ πλούσιον ὡς πτωχὸν θρηνωδοῦντα.
Μισῶ τὸν πτωχὸν καυχώμενον ἐν πλούτῳ.
Μισῶ χρεώστην ἀμερίμνως ὑπνοῦντα.
Μισῶ κολοβὸν μακρὸν ἐξουθενοῦντα.
10 Μισῶ τὸν μακρόν, ἂν πελωλὸς τυγχάνῃ.
Μισῶ τὸν ψεύστην σεμνυνόμενον λόγοις.
Μισῶ μέθυσον πίνοντα καὶ διψῶντα.
Μισῶ τὸν λίχνον ὡς ὀλιγοψιχοῦντα.
Μισῶ γέροντα παίζοντα μετὰ νέων.
15 Μισῶ ῥάθυμον καὶ τὸν ὑπνώδη μᾶλλον.
Μισῶ τὸν ἀναίσχυντον ἐν παρρησίᾳ.
Μισῶ τὸν πολυλόγον ἐν ἀκαιρίᾳ.
Μισῶ σιωπήν, ὅτε καιρὸς τοῦ λέγειν
Μισῶ τὸν πᾶσι συμμορφούμενον τρόποις.

Metre of Kassia in Iambic Verse

I HATE

I HATE a murderer condemning the hot-
tempered.
I HATE the adulterer when he judges
the fornicator.
I HATE the leper who drives out the
leprous.
I HATE the fool supposing to be a
philosopher.
5   I HATE a judge who takes orders from
individuals.
I HATE a rich man complaining as a
poor man.
I HATE the poor man boasting as in
wealth.
I HATE a debtor who sleeps
unconcernedly.
I HATE a stunted individual who is
contemptuous of height.
10   I HATE the tall man if he happens to
be enormous.
I HATE the liar affecting a solemn air
with words.
I HATE the drunk drinking and
thirsting.
I HATE the gluttonous one as he lacks
courage.
I HATE an old man who plays with
youths.
15   I HATE a lazy person and more so the
somnolent one.
I HATE the shameless individual in
candid speech.
I HATE the verbose in an unsuitable
time.
I HATE silence, when it is a time for
speaking.
I HATE the one who conforms to all
ways.

20   Μισῶ τὸν δόξης χάριν ποιοῦντα πάντα.
        Μισῶ τὸν λόγοις οὐκ ἀλείφοντα πάντασ.
        Μισῶ μὴ ζητούμενον καὶ προσλαλοῦντα.
        Μισῶ τὸν διδάσκοντα μηδὲν εἰδότα.
        Μισῶ φίλεχθρον οὐ γὰρ φιλεῖ τὸ θεῖον.
25   Μισῶ φειδωλὸν καὶ μάλιστα πλουτοῦντα.
        Μισῶ τὸν ἀγνώμονα καθὼς Ἰούδαν.
        Μισῶ τὸν μάτην συκοφαντοῦντα φίλους.

20   I HATE the one who does everything for
the sake of vain glory.
I HATE the one who does not encourage
everyone with words.
I HATE one who speaks before
examining.
I HATE the one who teaches knowing
nothing.
I HATE a quarrelsome one; for he does
not respect the holy.

25   I HATE the miser and especially one
who is wealthy.
I HATE the ungrateful one like Judas.
I HATE one who rashly slanders
friends.

Οἱ Ἀρμένιοι

Τῶν Ἀρμενίων τὸ δεινότατον γένος
ὕπουλόν ἐστι καὶ φαυλῶδες εἰς ἄγαν,
μανιῶδές τε καὶ τρεπτὸν καὶ βασκαῖνον,
πεφυσιωμένον πάμπλειστα καὶ δόλου
πλῆρες·
5   εἶπέ τις σοφὸς περὶ τούτων εἰκότως·
Ἀρμένιοι φαῦλοι μὲν, κἂν ἀδοξῶσι,
φαυλότεροι δὲ γίνονται δοξασθέντες,
πλουτήσαντες δὲ φαυλότατοι καθόλου,
ὑπερπλουτισθέντες {δὲ} καὶ τιμηθέντες
10   φαυλεπιφαυλότατοι δείκνυνται πᾶσι.

Disparaging remarks about the Armenians were
common among the Greeks of the Byzantine world during
the late eighth and ninth centuries, and the
terminology used is similar to that used in this
epigram. Cf. K. Krumbacher, Kasia Sitzungsberichte
der philosophish-philologischen und historischen
Klasse, III (Munich: Akademie der Wissenschaften,
1897), pp. 336-37. Armenians had long been an
ethnical constituent of the Empire, and a few had
occupied important positions, but in the ninth
century large numbers of them gained social and
political prominence. The officers and soldiers of
the army were mainly Armenians and were iconoclastic
by conviction. The iconodule tendencies of the Greek
Orthodox appeared to them to be idolatrous, and they
felt justified in using any kind of violence against
them. In the imperial ranks, the Emperors Leo V
(813-20) and Basil I (867-86), and the Empress
Theodora (842-56) were of Armenian descent. The
Patriarchs of Constantinople, John the Grammarian (c.
833-42), a staunch iconoclast, and Photius (858-69)
were also of Armenian descent. In addition to rising
to high rank and office in the Imperial service, the
Armenians were energetic, ambitious, and extremely
competitive, traits that soon made them very
successful in the fields of commerce and trade. The
Greek Byzantine world, especially the educated class,
resented and slighted the Armenians because of their
political influence and control in the Empire, their
iconoclastic views, and their competitiveness and
success in business.

The Armenians

The most powerful race of the
    Armenians
is sly and excessively villainous,
raging mad, unreliable and slanderous
they are extremely conceited and full
    of tricks.
5   A certain wise man appropriately said
    of them;
the Armenians are wicked, if they are
    held in low esteem,
but they become more wicked when they
    are highly regarded,
when they become wealthy, they are on
    the whole the most wicked,
and when they are exceedingly wealthy
    and honored
10   they show in every way that they are
    the worst that it is possible to
    be.

Ἀνὴρ

Ἀνὴρ φαλακρὸς καὶ κωφὸς καὶ μονόχειρ,
μογγίλαλός τε καὶ κολοβὸς καὶ μέλας,
λοξὸς τοῖς ποσὶ καὶ τοῖς ὄμμασιν ἅμα
ὑβρισθεὶς παρά τινος μοιχοῦ καὶ
πόρνου,
5   μεθυστοῦ, κλέπτου καὶ ψεύστου καὶ
φονέως
περὶ τῶν αὐτῷ συμβεβηκότων ἔφη·
Ἐγὼ μὲν οὐκ αἴτιος τῶν συμβαμάτων·
οὐ γὰρ θέλων πέφυκα τοιοῦτος ὅλως·
σὺ δὲ τῶν σαυτοῦ παραίτιος πταισμάτων·
10 ἅπερ γὰρ οὐκ ἔλαβες παρὰ τοῦ πλάστου,
ταῦτα καὶ ποιεῖς καὶ φέρεις καὶ
βαστάζεις.

Ἀνὴρ ἀληθὴς ἐκφεύγει πάντως ὅρκον.

Ἀνδρὸς ἀληθοῦς ὁ λόγος ὥσπερ ὅρκος·
ἀνδρὸς δὲ φαύλου καὶ τὸ ψεῦδος μεθ'
ὅρκου.

15 Ἀνὴρ στοχαστὴς μάντις ἄριστός ἐστιν·
τεκμαίρεται κινδύνους ἐκ τῶν
πραγμάτων.

Ἀνὴρ φρόνιμος ἐπικρατὴς ἀφρόνων,
αὐτπκράτωρ δὲ τῶν παθῶν ὁ τοιοῦτος.

Ἀνὴρ ὑψαύχην μισητὸς τοῖς ὁρῶσιν,
20 ἐπέραστος δὲ τοῖς πᾶσι ταπεινόφρων.

MAN

A man bald, dumb, and with only one
    hand,
short, swarthy, and with a speech
    impediment,
bowed legged and with crossed eyes
when he was insulted by a certain
    adulterer and fornicator,
5   drunk, thief, liar, and murderer
because of his infirmities, said:
"I am not the cause of my misfortunes;
for in no way did I want to be like
    this,
but you are in part the cause of your
    faults,
10   as you did not receive from the
    creator
these things that you do, endure, and
    dignify."

An honest man avoids all oaths.

The word of an honest man is like an
    oath;
but of an evil man even the lie is
    with an oath.

15   A keenly perceptive man is an
    excellent seer;
he recognizes dangers from
    circumstances.

A prudent man has mastery over the
    foolish,
such a man is ruler of the passions.

A stately man is hated by his viewers,
20   handsome but humble to all.

Φειδωλὸς ἰδὼν τὸν φίλον ἀπεκρύβη
καὶ τοὺς οἰκέτας τὸ ψεύδεσθαι
διδάσκει.

Φεύγει φειδωλὸς συμπόσια τῶν φίλων.

Φειδωλὸς ἅπας φίλους πτωχοὺς βαρεῖται.

Πλοῦτος/Πενία

Πλουτῶν πλήθυνον τοὺς φίλους ἐκ τοῦ
    πλούτου,
ἵνα σου πτωχεύσαντος μὴ ἐκσπασθῶσιν.

Πλοῦτος ἐπικάλυμμα κακῶν μεγίστων,
ἡ δὲ πτωχεία πᾶσαν γυμνοῖ κακίαν.

5   Κρεῖσσον πτωχεύειν ἢ πλουτεῖν ἐξ
        ἀδίκων.

Πλοῦτον μὴ ζήτει, μηδ' αὖ πάλιν
    πενίαν·
ὁ μὲν γὰρ τὸν νοῦν φυσιοῖ καὶ τὴν
    γνῶσιν,
ἡ δὲ τὴν λύπην ἀκατάπαυστον ἔχει.

10   Ὁ πλοῦτον ἔχων καὶ μὴ διδοὺς ἐτέρῳ,
    ἐν οἷς εὐτυχεῖ, δυστυχεῖ δηλονότι
    εἰς ψυχικὸν φυλάττων ὄλεθρον τοῦτον.
    ὁ δ' αὖ πενίαν εὐχαριστίᾳ φέρων
    δυστυχῶν εὐτύχησεν εἰς τὸν αἰῶνα.

A miser seeing his friend hides from
        sight
and teaches his household to lie.

A miser avoids the entertainment of
        friends.

A miser depresses all his poor
        friends.

        WEALTH/POVERTY

When you become wealthy, increase your
        friends with your wealth,
so that if you become poor, they might
        not fall away.

Wealth covers the greatest of evils,
but poverty strips all evil naked.

5   It is better to be poor than to be
        rich unjustly.

Don't seek wealth, or for that matter
        poverty;
for one inflates the mind and
        judgment,
the other brings unending grief.

One who has wealth and does not give
        to another,
10   is unfortunate in what he prospers,
        namely,
in mental anguish maintaining his
        wealth.
But one who endures poverty gracefully
being unfortunate he has succeeded
        forever.

Γυνή

Γυνὴ μοχθερὰ καὶ φίλεργος καὶ σώφρων
τὴν δυστυχίαν νενίκηκε προδήλως·
γυνὴ δὲ νωθρὰ καὶ μίσεργος καὶ φαύλη
τὴν κακὴν ὄντως ἐπεσπάσατο μοῖραν.

5   Φῦλον γυναικῶν ὑπερισχύει πάντων·
καὶ μάρτυς Ἔσδρας μετὰ τῆς ἀληθείας.

Κακὸν ἡ γυνὴ κἂν ὡραία τῷ κάλλει·
τὸ γὰρ κάλλος κέκτηται παραμυθίαν·
εἰ δ' αὖ δυσειδὴς καὶ κακότροπος εἴη,
10 διπλοῦν τὸ κακὸν παραμυθίας ἄτερ.

Μέτριον κακὸν γυνὴ φαιδρὰ τῇ θέᾳ,
ὅμως παρηγόρημα τὸ κάλλος ἔχει·
εἰ δ' αὖ καὶ γυνὴ καὶ δύσμορφος
    ὑπάρχοι,
φεῦ τῆς συμφορᾶς, φεῦ κακῆς
    εἱμαρμένης.

Κάλλος

Ρανίδα τύχης εἰκότως αἱρετέον
ἢ κάλλος μορφῆς ἄγαν ἐξηρημένον.

Χάριν κεκτῆσθαι κρεῖττον παρὰ κυρίου
ἤπερ ἀχαρίτωτον κάλλος καὶ πλοῦτον.

5   Κάλλος πέφυκεν εὔχροια πρὸ τῶν ὅλων,
ἔπειτα μερῶν καὶ μελῶν συμμετρία.

WOMAN

A woman industrious and prudent,
    although in hard times,
definitely overcomes her misfortunes;
but a woman lazy, idle, and mean,
actually causes misfortune.

5   Esdras is witness that women
    together with truth prevail over all.

It is not good for a woman to be
    beautiful;
for beauty is distracting;
but if she is ugly and ill mannered,
10   without distraction it is twice as
    bad.

It is moderately bad for a woman to
    have a radiant countenance,
yet beauty has its consolation;
but if a woman is ugly,
what misfortune, what bad luck.

lines 5-6. The reference is to the Old
Testament Apocryphal book of I Esdras 3:10-12;
4:13-32.

BEAUTY

One should prefer a drop of luck
than great beauty.

It is better to possess grace from the
    Lord,
than beauty and wealth that does not
    gain grace.

5   First comes beauty of countenance,
and then a well-proportioned body and
    limbs.

Φθόνος

῭Ωσπερ ἔχιδνα ῥήσσει τὴν τετοκυῖαν,
οὕτως ὁ φθόνος τὸν φθονοῦντα ῥηγνύει.
᾿Αρχὴ τοῦ φθόνου τῶν καλῶν εὐτυχία·
μηδὲν κερδαίνων ὁ φθόνος (ἀποκάμνει).

5   ᾿Ανδρὸς φθονεροῦ μέμηνεν ἡ καρδία.

῭Εξελε πᾶς τις τοῦ φθόνου τὸ
        στοιχεῖον·
(τὸν) θάνατόν φημι καὶ φέρει τοῦτον
        φθόνος·
πολλοῖς γὰρ συμβέβηκεν ἐκ φθόνου
        φόνος.

10   Φθόνε κάκιστε, τίς ὁ τεκών σε, φράσον,
       καὶ τίς ὁ πατάσσων σε καὶ διαρρήσσων;
       ᾿Εμὲ τέτοκε πάντως κενοδοξία,
       πατάσσει δε με φιλαδελφία δῆλον,
       διχάζει δέ με θεοῦ φόβος εἰς τέλος
       καὶ διαρρήσσει ταπείνωσις εἰς ἄπαν.

15   Φθονεῖν μὴ δῶς μοι, Χριστέ, μέχρι
        θανάτου,
       τὸ δὲ φθονεῖσθαι δός μοι ποθῶ γὰρ
        τοῦτο,
       τὸ δὲ φθονεῖσθαι πάντως ἐν ἔργοις
        θείοις.

       Πᾶς μνησίκακος καὶ φθονερὸς προδήλως·
       γεννήτρια γὰρ μνησικακία φθόνου.

ENVY

Just as a viper tears apart the one
    who bore it,
so envy tears apart the envious one.

The success of the accomplished is a
    cause for envy;
envy fails, gains nothing.

5   The heart of the envious man rages
    with wrath.

Drive out every rudiment of envy;
I believe envy even brings death;
For murder from envy has happened to
    many.

Tell, most evil envy, who bore you
10   and who can smite and destroy you?
Vanity definitely has borne me,
brotherly love surely smites me,
fear of God completely tears me apart,
and humility totally destroys me.

15   Christ, until death, let me not be
    envious,
but let me be envied; this I desire,
to be envied at least for good deeds.

All who bear malice and envy are
    obvious;
for malice is the parent of envy.

Μωρός

Οὐκ ἔστι μωρῷ φάρμακον τὸ καθόλου
οὐδὲ (καὶ) βοήθεια πλὴν τοῦ θανάτου.
μωρὸς τιμηθεὶς κατεπαίρεται πάντων,
ἐπαινεθεὶς δὲ θρασύνεται (καὶ) πλέον.
5   ὡς γὰρ ἄπορον κάμψαι κίονα μέγαν,
οὕτως οὐδ' ἄνθρωπον μωρὸν μεταποιεῖς.

Γνῶσις ἐν μωρῷ πάλιν ἄλλη μωρία·
γνῶσις ἐν μωρῷ κώδων ἐν ρινὶ χοίρου.

Δεινὸν τὸν μωρὸν γνώσεώς τι μετέχειν·
10 ἦν (δὲ) καὶ δόξης, δεινότατον εἰς
    ἅπαν·
ἦν δὲ καὶ νέος ὁ μωρὸς καὶ δυνάστης,
παπαῖ καὶ ἰώ, φεῦ καὶ οὐαὶ καὶ πόποι.

Οἴμοι, κύριε, μωροῦ σοφιζομένου·
ποῦ τις τράποιτο; ποῦ βλέψοι; πῶς
    ὑποίσοι;

15 Μωρὸς πάντως πέφυκε περισσοπράκτωρ·
μωρὸς βαλὼν πέδιλα πανταχοῦ τρέχει.

Κρεῖσσον τῷ μωρῷ πάμπαν μὴ γεγεννῆσθαι
ἢ γεννηθέντα τῇ γῇ μὴ βηματίσαι,
ἀλλὰ συντόμως Ἅιδη παραπεμφθῆναι.

STUPIDITY

There is absolutely no cure for
    stupidity
nor help except for death.
A stupid person when honored is
    arrogant towards everyone,
and when praised becomes even more
    over-confident.
5   Just as it is impossible to bend a
    great pillar,
so it is to change a stupid person.

Knowledge in a stupid person is
    further stupidity;
knowledge in a stupid person is a bell
    on a pig's nose.

It is terrible for a stupid person to
    possess some knowledge;
10   and if he has an opinion, it's even
    worse;
but if a stupid man is young and in a
    position of power,
alas and woe and what a disaster.

Woe, oh lord, if a stupid person
    attempts to be clever;
where does one flee, where does one
    turn, how does one endure?

15   A stupid person is always inclined to
    overdo:
Putting on a pair of shoes he runs
    everywhere.

It is better if a stupid person is
    never born
but if born, may he not walk on the
    earth
but soon afterwards be sent to Hades.

20   Μωροῖς φρόνιμος συνδιάγειν οὐ σθένει·
      ἀτονήσει γὰρ τῇ τούτων ἀντιθέσει,
      ἢ πῶς τὴν τούτων θρασύτητα νικήσοι;
      Αἱρετώτερον φρονίμοις συμπτωχεύειν
      ἥπερ συμπλουτεῖν μωροῖς καὶ
         ἀπαιδεύτοις.
25   καὶ μοὶ δοίη γε Χριστὸς
         συγκακουχεῖσθαι
      φρονίμοις ἀνδράσι τε καὶ σοφωτάτοις
      ἥπερ συνευφραίνεσθαι μωροῖς ἀλόγοις.

20   An association between a sensible
                person and a stupid one cannot
                endure;
          for it will weaken by their
                antithesis,
          how can it overcome their impudence?
          It is better to be poor with sensible
                people
          than to be rich with stupid and
                ignorant ones.
25   May Christ grant me to endure
                adversity
          with sensible and prudent men
          than to rejoice together with
                irrational stupid ones.

Διάφορα

Πάντας δ' ἀγάπα μὴ θάρρει δὲ τοῖς
πᾶσιν.

Γάλα καὶ μέλι συγγενῶν ὁμιλίαι.

Σύνεσις παίδων γερόντων ὁμιλίαι.

Ἀσκανδάλιστος βίος ἢ πλοῦτος μέγας.

5   (Στοργὴ κολάκων ὡς γραπτὴ πανοπλία
πλανῶσιν (γὰρ) ὑμᾶς ἡδοναῖς
ἐπαινέται.)

Θυμὸς πέφυκε τῶν κακίστων τὸ πέρας
θυμὸς οὐ τιμᾷ φιλίαν, οὐκ αἰδεῖται.

10   Εὐημερῶν δ' ἐκδέχου καὶ δυστυχίαν
εἰς δυστυχίαν δ' ἐμπεσὼν γενναίως
φέρε.

Μόνος μονωθεὶς ὁ τὰς ὀδύνας ἔχων
διπλῆν ἔχει σκότωσιν καὶ ῥαθυμίαν.

Μέγα φάρμακον τοῖς πενθοῦσιν ὑπάρχει
τῶν συναλγούντων τὸ δάκρυον καὶ ῥῆμα.

15   Βάσανον ἔχει τὴν ζωὴν ὁ ἐν λύπαις.

MISCELLANEOUS

Love everyone, but don't trust all.

The company of family is like milk and
     honey.

The sagacity of children is the
     discussion of the old.

Better an inoffensive life than great
     wealth.

5   The affection of flatterers is like a
          painted suit of armor;
       for it commends you with deceptive
          delights.

Anger generates the worst of evils;
anger neither honors friendship, nor
     is ashamed.

Be happy but also expect misfortune;
10   and if you fall into misfortune endure
       it nobly.

A solitary man when abandoned has a
     twofold distress;
he suffers from both gloom and
     indifference.

A powerful remedy for those in
     mourning
is the tears and word of those sharing
     in their sorrow.

15   A person in distress considers life a
          trial.

Εἰ τὸ φέρον σε φέρει, φέρου καὶ φέρε·
εἰ δὲ τὸ φέρον σε φέρει καὶ σὺ οὐ
    φέρεις,
σαυτὸν κακώσεις καὶ τὸ φέρον σε φέρει.

Πρὸς κέντρα μὴ λάκτιζε γυμνοῖς ποσί
    σου·
20   ἐπεὶ τὰ κέντρα μηδαμῶς καταβλάψας
σαυτὸν τρώσειας καὶ πόνον ὑποστήσῃ.

Κρεῖσσον μόνωσις τῆς κακῆς συνουσίας.

Κρεῖσσον καὶ νόσος τῆς κακῆς εὐεξίας.

Κρεῖσσον ἀσθενεῖ ἢ κακῶς ὑγιαίνειν.

25   Κρεῖσσον σιωπᾶν ἢ λαλεῖν ἃ μὴ θέμις.
ἐκ σιωπῆς γὰρ οὐ κίνδυνος, οὐ μῶμος,
οὐ μετάμελος, οὐκ ἔγκλησις, οὐχ ὅρκος.

Μέγα τὸ κέρδος τῆς καλῆς συμμετρίας.

Εἰ μισεῖς τὸ ψέγεσθαι, τινὰ μὴ ψέξῃς.

30   Πᾶς πολύορκος εἰς ψευδορκίαν πίπτει.

If destiny bears you, bear with it and
be bourn;
but if destiny bears you and you do
not bear with it,
you harm yourself, but destiny still
bears you.

Don't kick against the pricks with
your bare feet;
20   since you can't damage the pricks in
any way
you will only hurt yourself and be in
pain.

Solitude is better than bad company.

Illness is better than poor ability.

It is better to be needy than to fare
poorly.

25   It is better to be silent than to
speak of things that are not
lawful:
for there is no danger from silence,
no blame,
no regret, no accusation, no oath.

There is great gain from harmony.

If you hate blame, don't blame anyone.

30   Anyone who swears a lot falls into
perjury.

lines 16-18. Cf: Palladas' epigrams 10:73 in
The Greek Anthology, Vol. IV, ed. W. R. Paton, Loeb
Classics (Cambridge: Harvard University Press,
1956).

lines 19-21. Cf: Acts 9:5, don't hurt yourself
by useless resistance.

Κακὸν ὀμόσαι, χεῖρον ἐπιορκῆσαι.

Χρὴ παντάπασι φυλάττεσθαι τὸν ὅρκον.

Πᾶς φιλόνεικος πληθύνει καὶ τοὺς
    ὅρκους ·
πᾶς φιλόνεικος καὶ θυμὸν συνεισφέρει.

35   Ἐν δ' ἀμφιβόλοις νεύει πᾶς τις
    ἐχέφρων.
    (καὶ φεύγει πάμπαν τοὺς ἐχθραίνοντας
    μάτους.)

    (Εὐρὼν δυστυχὴς χρυσίον εἶλε τοῦτο
    καὶ γέγονε κίνδυνος ἐκ τούτου τούτῳ ·
    ὁ δ' εὐτυχής, κἂν ὅφιν εὕρῃ ζῶντα,
40   εἰς ὅφελος γίνεται τούτῳ καὶ κέρδος.)

    Σπάνιόν ἐστι τοῦ ἀγαθοῦ ἡ κτῆσις,
    τοῦ δ' αὖ γε κακοῦ λίαν εὐχερεστάτη.

    Δυστυχὴς ἅπας ἐν πᾶσι κονδυλίζει,
    τῷ δ' εὐτυχεῖ πέφυκεν εὐθὺ τὰ πάντα.

45   Περιστάσεσιν ἐμπίπτων μὴ ἐκλύου ·
    πάντως γὰρ οὐδὲν θεοῦ πάθοιμεν δίχα.

    Ὑβριζόμενος καὶ τὰ ἴσα μὴ λέγων
    σοφὸς δειχθήσῃ καὶ φρόνιμος εἰς ἄγαν.

    Ἀπαιδευσίας μήτηρ ἡ παρρησία ·
50   παρρησία λέγεται παρὰ τὸ ἴσον ·
    πέρα γάρ ἐστι τοῦ ἴσου καὶ τοῦ μέτρου.

It is wrong to confirm by oath, worse
    to swear falsely.

It is absolutely necessary to keep an
    oath.

Every contentious individual also
    multiplies oaths;
every contentious individual
    improperly uses anger.

35   Any sensible person when in doubt
completely avoids suspicious
    pursuits.

An unlucky person when he finds a
    piece of silver, seizes it
and incurs danger from it;
but for a lucky person, even a
    live snake
40   becomes a profit and gain for him.

The possession of good is rare,
but on the other hand evil is
    very available.

An unfortunate man finds every
    difficulty in all things,
but to a fortunate one everything
    immediately falls into place.

45   Falling upon difficult situations,
    don't despair;
for nothing happens to us without the
    will of God.

When insulted and maligned,
a wise person will behave very
    sensibly.

Excess is the mother of ignorance;
50   excessiveness means contrary to equal
    balance
for it is beyond equality and
    moderation.

Ἤνεγκέ μοί τι κέρδος ἡ δυσπραξία,
ὥσπερ τὸν χρυσὸν ἐν πυρὶ δοκιμάζεις.
Φύσις πονερὰ χρηστὸν ἦθος οὐ τίκτει.
55   Κρεῖσσον ἀληθῶς ἐπιφυλλὶς δικαίου
ἤπερ τρυγητὸς ἀσεβῶν παρανόμων.
Κρεῖσσον ἡττᾶσθαι τοῦ νικᾶν ἀπεικότως.
Κρεῖσσον ὀλίγον καλὸν ἐξ εὐνομίας
ἢ τὸ πολλοστὸν ἀπὸ παρανομίας.
60   Κακοῖς συνεῖναι πάμπαν οὐκ ἐξισχύει
ὁ κεκτημένος μισοπόνηρον γνώμην.

Ἐνεργείᾳ μὲν τῶν πονηρῶν δαιμόνων,
τῇ τοῦ θεοῦ δὲ πάντως παραχωρήσει
κακοποιοῦσιν οἱ κακοὶ τοὺς βελτίους
65   πρὸς τὸ δειχθῆναι τούτους
      εὐριζοτέρους.

Τῆς λ<αθροβού>λ<ου> κρείττων ἀγάπης
     μάχη ·
φυλάττεται γὰρ πᾶς τις ἐκ τῆς
     δευτέρας,
εἰς δὲ τὴν πρώτην πλανηθεὶς * σι *.

Πᾶν τὸ βιασθὲν τάχος ἐκκλίνει πάλιν,
70   τὸ δ' αὖ φυσικὸν καὶ μόνιμον ὑπάρχει.

Ῥᾴδιόν ἐστι τὸ κακὸν τοῦ βελτίου ·
τὸ γὰρ ἀγαθὸν ἔοικεν ἀναφόρῳ,
τὸ δ' αὖ πονηρὸν οἷον τῷ κατηφόρῳ ·
καὶ πᾶς τις οἶδε, πόσον κατωφορίζειν
75   εὐκοπώτερον ἤπερ ἀναφορίζειν.

Ποθεῖς ἐπαίνους ἐπαινετέα πρᾶττε!

Tell me of what advantage is bad luck;
it's like testing gold in the fire.

A wicked nature does not engender good
    moral character.

55 The discarded grapes of a just man are
        truly better
    than the vintage of an unjust and
        profane one.

It is better to be defeated than to
    win unfairly.

A little gain obtained legally
is better than much gotten illegally.

60 It is not possible for someone
    who hates dishonesty to associate with
        evil persons.

When confronted with the activity of
    evil powers,
    that of God will withdraw completely;
    the bad will harm the good
65 in order to show that they are more
        strongly established.

Strife is better than a secret love;
for everyone guards against the one,
but wanders into the other....

Any thing forced deteriorates again
    quickly,
70 but what comes naturally lasts.

Evil is easier than good;
for the good is like a steep ascent,
but evil is more a declivity;
and everyone knows how much easier
75 it is to descend than to ascend.

Do you wish praise; act praiseworthy!

line 68. The last word of the epigram is
unreadable due to a rip in the manuscript.

Περὶ μοναχῶν

Μοναχός ἐστιν ἑαυτὸν μόνον ἔχων.
Μοναχός ἐστι μονολόγιστος βίος.
Μοναχὸς ἔχων βιωτικὰς φροντίδας
οὗτος πολλοστός, οὐ μοναχὸς κεκλήσθω.
5   Μοναχοῦ βίος κουφότερος ὀρνέου.
Μοναχοῦ βίος περιεργίας ἄνευ.
Μοναχοῦ βίος εἰρηνικὸς διόλου.
Μοναχοῦ βίος ἀτάραχος καθάπαξ.
Μοναχοῦ βίος ἡσύχιος διόλου.
10 Μοναχός ἐστι πεπαιδευμένη γλῶττα.
Μοναχός ἐστι μὴ πλανώμενον ὄμμα.
Μοναχός ἐστι νοῦς κατεστηριγμένος.
Μοναχός ἐστιν ἀπαράνοικτος θύρα.
Μοναχός ἐστι στηριγμὸς ἀστηρίκτων.
15 Μοναχός ἐστι καθίστορον βιβλίον
δεικνύον ὁμοῦ τοὺς τύπους καὶ
διδάσκον.
Βίος μοναστοῦ λύχνος φαίνων τοῖς πᾶσι.
Βίος <μονα>στοῦ ὁδηγὸς πλανωμένων.
Βίος μοναστοῦ φυγαδευτὴς δαιμόνων.
20 Βίος μοναστοῦ θερα<π>ευτὴς ἀγγέλων.
Βίος μοναστοῦ πρὸς δόξαν θεοῦ μόνου.
Τάξις ἀρίστη τοῦ παντὸς ἀρχομένου
<καὶ> τελειοῦντος πᾶν ἔργον τε καὶ
ῥῆμα
θεὸν ποιεῖσθαι τὴν ἀρχὴν καὶ τὸ τέλος.

_____

Monachos is the term used to describe anyone
living a monastic life, a life of denial of all
earthly things and in total devotion to and
contemplation of God. Such a person could be either
a member of a monastic community or living as a
hermit. These epigrams on the monastic life are
modeled after those of Theodore the Studite abbot
(759-826), who wrote a series of epigrams on the
various aspects of the monastic life and community
that were copied and imitated for many years. Like
Theodore, Kassia celebrates the monastic life as a
noble one of self-denial, quiet acceptance of
suffering and poverty, and contemplation of God. It
is a life of total renouncement of the world and all
its cares and concerns. A monastic's only concern is
glorification of God and observance of Christ's

Concerning Monachoi

Monachos is having only yourself.
Monachos is a single-thought life.
Monachos having worldly concerns has
     been called
many names but not monachos.
5   Monachos' life is more unencumbered
        than that of a bird.
Monachos' life is without curiosity.
Monachos' life is always peaceful.
Monachos' life is absolute calm.
Monachos' life is always solidarity.
10 Monachos is a restrained tongue.
Monachos is a non-wandering eye.
Monachos is a firmly fixed mind.
Monachos is a completely shut door.
Monachos is a support of the
        unsupported.
15 Monachos is an established book,
showing the model to be imitated and
        teaching at the same time.
The life of a monastic is a lamp
        bringing light to all.
The life of a monastic is a guide to
        those led astray.
The life of a monastic is a banisher
        of demons.
20 The life of a monastic is a servant of
        the angels.
The life of a monastic is devoted
        solely to the glorification of
        God.
The excellent order at the beginning
        of the whole
and the completion of every word and
        deed
postulates God the beginning and the
        end.

precepts. As lines 38-39 state, an individual that
has attained such a state, lives a life of continuous
spiritual joy and celebration. These epigrams
express in a simple, straightforward manner Kassia's
views of the monastic life.

Τί εἶναι μοναχός

Σήμερον ἐν τῷ κόσμῳ
καὶ αὔριον ἐν τῷ ταφῳ:-
μνήμη θανάτον, χρησιμεύει τῷ βίῳ.

Μοναχὸς ἐστὶ νοῦς ἠγνισμένος
5 καὶ κεκαθαρμένον στόμα.

Μοναχὸς ἐστὶ τάξις καὶ κατά-
στασις ἀσωμάτων ἐν σώματι ὑλικῷ
καὶ ρυπαρῷ ἐκτελουμένη.

Μοναχὸς ἐστίν, ἄγγελος ἐπίγειος ἐξόχως
10 τε καὶ κυρίως καὶ ἄνθρωπος οὐράνιος.

Μοναχὸς ἐστίν, ὁ μένων ἄχρι τέλους
τῇ τε κακοπαθείᾳ καὶ τοῖς λυπηροῖς,
εἴγε ἄχος ἐστι λύπη, ἀφωνίαν
ἐμποιοῦσα.

15 Μοναχὸς ἐστίν, λήθη παντελὴς
καὶ ἀναισθησία τῶν καταρθουμένων.

Μοναχὸς ἐστίν, οἶκος Θεοῦ, καθέδρα
βασιλική, παλάτιον τῆς ἁγίας Τριάδος.

Μοναχὸς ἐστίν, ἀπόκρυφος νοῦς.

20 Μοναχὸς ἐστὶ κιθάρα πνευματικὴ
ὄργανον
ἀνακρουόμενον ἐμμελῶς.

What is a Monachos?

Today in the world
and tomorrow in the grave,
the thought of death consumes life.

5   Monachos is a purified mind
and a cleansed mouth.

Monachos is order and a state
of bodilessness achieved in a
material and unpurged body.

Monachos is above all, an earthly
        angel
10   and in control; a godly man.

Monachos is one who throughout misery
and painful situations, if pain is
really a sad plight, remains
silent.

15   Monachos is a complete forgetting
and indifference to accomplishments.

Monachos is a house of God, a royal
throne, palace of the Holy Trinity.

Monachos is a concealed mind.

20   Monachos is a spiritual lyre, an
instrument harmoniously played.

Μοναχὸς ἐστί, πάλη σαρκός, κατὰ τὸ
εἰρημένον, οὐκ ἔστιν ἡμῖν ἡ πάλη
πρὸς αἷμα καὶ σάρκα   νόει τὸ ρητὸν
25   καὶ μὴ παράτρεχε   τοῦτο γὰρ καὶ
πολλῆς δεῖται τῆς προσοχῆς.

Μοναχὸς ἐστίν, ὃς οὐ φοβεῖται τὸν
Θεόν,
ἀλλ' ἀγαπᾷ αὐτόν   ἡ γὰρ τελεία
ἀγάπη ἔξω ρίπτει τὸν φόβον.
30   Μοναχὸς ἐστί, νεκρὸς περιπατῶν.

Μοναχὸς ἐστί, θνῆσις ἐκούσιος κόσμου.

Μοναχὸς ἐστὶν ἐκεῖνος, ὁ ἀεὶ ἀναβάσεις
ἐν τῇ καρδίᾳ διατιθέμενος.

Μοναχὸς ἐστίν, ἐκούσιος δίψα, μόνα
35   διψῶν τὰ οὐράνια   καὶ πρὸς τὰ
μέλλοντα χάριτι τοῦ Παναγάθου Θεοῦ
τὸν νοῦν ἐντεῦθεν ἀπάρας. Ξένην
δεὶ ἑορτὴν ὁ τοιοῦτος πανηγυρίζει
τε καὶ ἑορτάζει   μακάριος ὁ τούτου
40   τυχών   ἐκεῖνος μόνος οἶδεν ἑτέρους
διδάξαι τε καὶ φωτίσαι καὶ πρὸς
τὴν βασιλείαν καθοδηγῆσαι ἐν Χριστῷ
Ἰησοῦ τῷ Κυρίῳ ἡμῶν, μεθ' ὅν τῷ
Πατρὶ σὺν ἁγίῳ Πνεύματι.

45   Μοναχὸς ἐστὶ φιλία νηστείας ἔχθρα τῶν
ἡδωνῶν (sic).
Μοναχὸς ἐστί, μῖσος παθῶν, ἀγάπη καλῶν
Μοναχὸς ἐστίν, εὖχος χριστιανῶν.

line 45.   ἡδωνῶν should be ἡδονῶν.

Monachos is a struggle with the flesh,
   as it
has been stated, to me the struggle is
   not
with blood and flesh; know the
   Scriptures
25   and don't treat them cursorily, for it
   is this
   that is in need of much attention.

Monachos is one who does not fear God
but loves him; for complete love
casts out fear.

30   Monachos is a walking corpse.

Monachos is a voluntary death of the
   world.

Monachos is one who, in his heart, is
always disposed to the spiritual
   ascents.

Monachos is voluntary thirst,
35   thirsting only after the heavenly
and the things to come through grace
of the absolutely good God; therefore
   his
mind is lifted high. Such an
   individual always
attends and celebrates a wonderful
   festival;
40   blessed is he who succeeds in this.
He alone knows how to teach and
   enlighten others
and lead them to the Kingdom of Jesus
Christ our Lord, who is with the
Father and with the Holy Spirit.

45   Monachos is a friend of fasting, enemy
   of pleasure.
Monachos is hatred of the passions,
   love of the good.
Monachos is the pride of the
   Christians.

Indices

FIRST LINE INDICES

Greek

145

English

The Garland Library of Medieval Literature

72. Mechthild von Magdeburg: *Flowing Light of the Divinity*. Translated by Christiane Mesch Galvani; edited, with an introduction, by Susan Clark. Series B.

73. Robert de Boron: *The Grail Trilogy*. Translated by George Diller. Series B.

74. *Till Eulenspiegel: His Adventures*. Translated, with introduction and notes, by Paul Oppenheimer. Series B.

75. Francesco Petrarch: *Rime Disperse*. Edited and translated by Joseph Barber. Series A.

76. Guillaume de Deguileville: *The Pilgrimage of Human Life (Le Pèlerinage de la vie humaine)*. Translated by Eugene Clasby. Series B.

77. Renaut de Bâgé: *Le Bel Inconnu (Li Biaus Descouneüs; The Fair Unknown)*. Edited by Karen Fresco; translated by Colleen P. Donagher; music edited by Margaret P. Hasselman. Series A.

78. Thomas of Britain: *Tristran*. Edited and translated by Stewart Gregory. Series A.

79. *Kudrun*. Translated by Marion E. Gibbs and Sidney M. Johnson. Series B.

80. *A Thirteenth-Century Life of Charlemagne*. Translated by Robert Levine. Series B.

81. Penninc and Pieter Vostaert: *Roman van Walewein*. Edited and translated by David F. Johnson. Series A.

82. *Medieval Literature of Poland: An Anthology*. Translated by Michael J. Mikoś. Series B.

83. *Helyas or Lohengrin: Late Medieval Transformations of the Swan Knight Legend*. Edited and translated by Salvatore Calomino. Series A.

84. *Kassia: The Legend, the Woman, and Her Work*. Edited and translated by Antonía Tripolitis. Series A.

85. *The Song of Aliscans*. Translated by Michael A. Newth. Series B.

86. *The Vows of the Heron (Les Voeux du héron): A Middle French Vowing Poem*. Edited by John Grigsby and Norris J. Lacy; translated by Norris J. Lacy. Series A.

87. *Medieval Galician-Portuguese Poetry: An Anthology*. Edited and translated by Frede Jensen. Series A.

88. *Jaufre: An Occitan Arthurian Romance*. Translated by Ross G. Arthur. Series B.

89. Hildegard of Bingen's *The Book of the Rewards of Life (Liber Vitae Meritorum)*. Translated by Bruce Hozeski. Series B.

90. Brunetto Latini: *The Book of the Treasure (Le Livre du Tresor)*. Translated by Paul Barrette and Spurgeon Baldwin. Series B.

91. The Pleier's Arthurian Romances: *Garel of the Blooming Valley, Tandareis and Flordibel, Meleranz*. Translated by J. W. Thomas. Series B.